MODERN FOOTBALL FOR THE SPECTATOR

BY THE AUTHOR OF

MODERN SINGLE WING FOOTBALL

Modern Football for the Spectator

by CHARLES W. CALDWELL, JR.

HEAD COACH

PRINCETON UNIVERSITY

*Illustrated with 60 diagrams
and figures and
16 pages of photographs*

J. B. LIPPINCOTT COMPANY

PHILADELPHIA AND NEW YORK

Library of Congress Card Catalog Number 53–8924

Contents

5

Contents

*Illustrations from photographs are grouped
following page 64*

Foreword

During my privileged years of association with the great modern game of football, I have discussed many phases of the game with spectators far and wide. Their lack of comprehension of the ever-changing progress of the game, the rules, the preparation behind the scenes and the actual strategy involved in the game, whether high school, college or professional, convinced me there was a need for this book.

Plans for presenting the following material resulted in many inquiries seeking the *middle road* of spectator knowledge. In the end I found that the range of understanding extended from the low of a fair damsel who attended games to "see the half-time show" to the high of a former coach who has forgotten more about football than I will ever know.

Consequently, many facts contained herein may be "old stuff" to some, but I sincerely hope that all who read this book will discover something new about the game which will increase their enjoyment and appreciation of the game of football at all levels regardless of the viewing medium.

I will be ever grateful to Dick Colman and John Stiegman of my coaching staff for their time and help with the technical material. Don Stuart, Sports Editor of the *Princeton Alumni Weekly*, Dan Coyle, Director of Athletic Publicity in the Princeton Department of Public Relations, and especially Bill Robinson, erudite Sports Writer of the *Newark Evening News,* have rendered invaluable counsel and assistance to earn my deep appreciation for their contribution.

CHARLIE CALDWELL

Princeton, N. J.
April 8, 1953

MODERN FOOTBALL FOR THE SPECTATOR

1 What Is Football?

On a recent autumn Saturday, a sportswriter returned to his home town from covering a football game and joined a dinner party made up of friends who had been spectators at another game that same afternoon, a much-publicized "big game" between undefeated old rivals, with a league title at stake and a sell-out crowd looking on.

It had been one of the memorable games of the year, and the people who had watched it were still bubbling with excitement. In a confused chorus they began to tell the sportswriter all about their wonderful afternoon. In the group were two former college players from the 1930's and a man who had been a student team manager as an undergraduate. All of them loved the game of football and loved the fun and excitement of afternoons spent in the stadium following their team.

Out of the confusion, the expert tried to glean some facts about the game. "Who made the touchdowns?" he asked.

There was a pause while everyone exchanged glances. There were a few timid guesses and finally a shrug.

"How did the winners ever keep the other team from scoring?"

This brought a burst of talk about pass interceptions, but no one was sure whether there was any special defense involved or whether it was just poor passing by the losing offense.

"Did the winning team stick to its regular Single Wing or did it go into the T every once in a while?" the sportswriter wanted to know. No one had the answer to this.

In other words, this group of fans, who could be called average, or above, in their knowledge of football, had missed many of the finer points of the contest, despite their intense interest.

The sportswriter happened to interview me the following week and told me his experience. The story made me wonder just how much the modern game of football had gotten beyond the ability of the average spectator to take it all in. It was something of a revelation, because we coaches had been so busily engaged in working on the sport, and so convinced that the modern game was a vast improvement over the way it had been played in the past, that we had perhaps failed to recognize the fact that we had left many of our most loyal and interested supporters behind in the process.

Perhaps the time had come for taking stock, a recap of just what the spectator should look for in watching a football game as it is played today. If the fans could be given a fuller realization of the organization of the game, its current terminology, its formations and alignments and the rules under which it is played, they should achieve a greater appreciation of the elements of the contest and enjoy a more rewarding experience through fuller understanding. Hence this book.

The roots of this difficulty experienced by present day spectators go back a long way. All the way, in fact, to November 6, 1869, when an informal collection of students from Rutgers and Princeton met on a field at New Brunswick, New Jersey, and spent the afternoon chasing a ball over the turf, to the confusion of a few casual onlookers. Thus was the game of football born in this country, and from that very first game the sport was marked for growth and development. As quickly as the next week, when the teams played a return match at Princeton, they showed better organization and an increased grasp of the problems involved in the game.

Football has never been static since. There have been constant growth and development in techniques. Rules have been changed, new systems devised and new uses thought up for the different positions, until the game of football as we know it today has emerged. An especially rapid era of change and development took place in the years immediately following World War II, when the extent of innovation exceeded that of any equal period of time in the past.

This era of greatest development may well have been ended by the rule change of January 1953 that sounded the death knell of the so-called "two platoon" system. The rule on substitutions in effect during the late 1940's and early 1950's allowed a coach to use complete and separate units on offense and defense as well as specialists for such functions as punting, passing, extra points and kicking off.

It was an unparalleled chance for coaches to work out techniques and sciences in these fields. Ideas that had been in the back of their minds, without previous chance for use, were developed and exploited. Each position and each function could now receive almost undivided attention. And so the specialist was born and nurtured until most football players were not well-rounded in all phases of the game but were skilled in their own specialties to a degree never before known in the sport.

This period has been dubbed with such nicknames as the "two-platoon age" and "age of the specialist," but it might also have been called the "coaches' era." It provided unprecedented opportunities for the coaching profession to innovate, alter, adapt, develop and change, all within the framework of the rules. The old adage of "anything worth doing at all is worth doing well" could be followed as never before.

The return to "one platoon" operations put a halt to the full exercise of these opportunities, but the developments made possible in the two-platoon era are now an accepted part of the game. They can no longer be used in exactly the same way, and some specialties are bound to suffer; but the way has been pointed to a more complete employment of an individual's faculties and to fuller exploitation of the possibilties in a situation.

Perhaps the end of this "coaches' era" has created an opportunity for the spectator to catch up with the game in all its ramifications. It is certain, though, that a fan who had not seen a game since the mid-'30's and was therefore considerably confused by two-platoon football, will not find the game returning to the style of that era simply through the 1953 rule change.

Football is a changed sport in its particulars if not in its fundamentals, and the end has certainly not been reached. The coaching profession has gone right to work on the problems of the "one-platoon" game and will always strive to improve the old and discover the new, developing ways of scoring with eleven men and a ball, or of preventing scoring with eleven men without a ball.

It is unfortunate if these refinements in the science of football have left some of its devotees behind, because the game still retains its basic appeal as a stirring contest. No other sport matches it in its combination of physical prowess and the mental fascination of chess or military strategy. An appreciation of the physical accomplishments of a team, the long runs, scoring passes, crisp blocks and smashing tackles that every spectator can see for himself, is only a part of the enjoyment that can be the reward of the football fan. When you go to a game, you should have equipped yourself with an understanding of the planning and techniques behind these end products: the "why?" as well as the "what?" of the situation.

This post-World War II period that saw such a rapid development in a sport that had by then a history of seventy-five years behind it, also saw many changes in the game's place in the sports pattern of the nation. After a temporary boom in the first seasons immediately following the war, attendance began to fall off and costs began to rise astronomically. An analysis of the reasons behind the attendance decline is not within the scope of this book, but it is safe to say that the impact of television had a lot to do with it.

As a result, many colleges, mostly those classed as "independents" or schools without league or conference affiliations, were forced to drop out of the sport, and, with few exceptions, the colleges still supporting football found a much tighter squeeze on their budgets. Since the majority of institutions use football receipts to finance the rest of their athletic program, this posed a threat to college athletics as a whole. Much serious thought has been given to the problem.

While attendance was dropping at the actual games, as a general trend, however, football was far from dropping in public interest. Television was the answer to this. Although games all across the country on a given Saturday might attract fewer people than in pre-television years, the sport was coming before countless new viewers electronically. Just as radio in the 1920's served to dramatize the game to sections of the public never before interested in it, so did television bring it before a new and expanded public.

In talking to the football public today, it is necessary to think of all three types of fans: those who still hear their game by radio, the television public, and the actual spectators at a game. The succeeding chapters of this book can be used as a guide for all three types though some of the subjects covered, naturally, cannot pertain to radio listening. Here you are dependent on the announcer and his spotters for an analysis of what your own eyes could tell you in the other two mediums. Since game action is fast and ever-changing, radio announcers are often unable to stop and explain. However, a familarity with what takes places in a game, as outlined here, can help you in following the radio announcer's rapid fire account.

Any remarks I might make about the relative merits of television versus the actual viewing of a game could be taken as prejudiced in view of the continuing controversy over the effect of video on the sport. However, there are some facts that can be brought out, without getting into the controversial side of the question, that should be of help to those who take their football at home.

Of primary importance is your dependence on some one else's "eyes" for what you are shown. As later chapters point out, there are certain places you should look before and during a game to achieve a full understanding of what has gone into a play. If the cameraman does not show you, you are helpless. He may be fooled by the play, or the omission may be due to physical limitations of the camera. One of our chapters is entitled "Don't Watch the Ball," in which we try to show you how to achieve a better grasp of the play through watching other areas of action. Yet since they are serving a broad public, including many viewers unfamiliar with the fine points of the game, television cameramen do concentrate on the ball as much as possible, cutting out many auxiliary details of play that should be noted for full appreciation of what goes on. This is a limitation that must be kept in mind when using this book as a guide to television viewing of football.

As for actual attendance at the stadium, no one can deny that you are subject to the inconveniences of weather and traffic, poor seats and surrounding distractions, not to mention cash out of pocket for the tickets, as opposed to a free show at home. You have, however, been able to choose the exact game you want to see, and you can benefit from the many facets television cameras cannot pick up. As we will show later on, observation of pre-game warm-up sessions and weather conditions, a study of the actions of the coaches and officials before the game begins and a mental participation in the first contest of the afternoon, the coin toss that starts the game, can add to your appreciation and understanding of the whole affair.

And we hope that, by the time you have absorbed what we have to say in this book, you will realize how many interesting and informative details an alert spectator can pick up about a game during its progress.

Since its very early days one of the big appeals of football has been its glamour as a spectacle. The phrase "perfect football weather" has become part of the language, meaning a crisp fall day, highlighted by nature's autumnal display of colors and tingling with the excitement of bands playing and crowds wending their way across a campus to the stadium.

For undergraduates, alumni, and their friends and family, it is a happy social occasion. Being part of an undergraduate cheering section creates a feeling of belonging, a bond of fellowship that is a big part of one's emotional loyalty to an institution. For alumni, returning to the campus awakens memories of happy student days and continues the tie that was established then. In addition to those directly connected with an institution, the game of football attracts a band of "stadium faithful," rabid fans who see a game every week, follow the coaches and players intently and are among a team's most ardent supporters. In big city areas, they are sometimes known as "subway alumni."

It is just this crowd appeal and glamour that has been responsible for some of the difficulties the sport has encountered in recent years. Because it has natural color and excitement, these very elements carry the seeds of serious problems for an amateur sport. There is a popular appeal about it that can lead to excesses of commercial exploitation and the attendant evils of proselytizing and the lowering of academic standards.

These unfortunate features of college football have received a great deal of attention in the post-war era. No one can deny they exist and that they are wrong. In the hue and cry of reform, however, there has been a tendency to overlook the positive values of the sport. If we coaches were not convinced of this positive value, you would find us engaged in some other more peaceful, less nerve-racking profession. The rewards of being connected with the game of football have to be very real in personal satisfaction to overcome the pressures and, all too often, the public scorn, to which the fraternity is exposed.

From your seat high in the stadium, the players and the contest take on a remote, impersonal aspect. Uniforms tend to add to the impersonal effect, and spectators have a tendency to forget the human elements involved. It is hard to think of the players as human beings, individuals with all the variety of facial features, coloring, voices, personal mannerisms, emotions and mental capacity you would find in any other group of youngsters of the same age. I use the word youngsters advisedly. It is hard to remember that most of the rugged-looking helmeted figures you see engaged in grid combat are not fully matured men. Most of them are still in their late teens or below voting age, not very far away from the emotional and physical uncertainties of adolescence.

Although thousands of people come to watch them perform, and press, radio and television coverage builds them up into figures of national prominence, they are still youths being trained for adulthood. Their hour in the spotlight on Saturday afternoons is brief, and the rest of their life is taken up with the normal activities of the age group, the classroom work, tests, library hours, letters from home and evening study. Football players do lead a life apart during the season, with training tables and practice periods taking them away from normal student haunts part of the time, but the fact that football is still a game for young men who are also engaged in the process of getting an education should never be forgotten.

It is when this fact is forgotten, or purposely overlooked, that the excesses outweigh the benefits of the game.

When football is kept in its proper perspective it can be of great value to players and spectators alike. As you will see during your trip behind the scenes in the ensuing chapters, the many ramifications of the sport are invaluable in the development in young men of many qualities that are needed for adult citizenship and leadership. The obvious ones of physical strength, courage and stamina are only part of the story. Even more important are the elements of discipline, team play, selfless cooperation, and loyalty. The ability to think under the double pressures of physical contact and psychological urgency is of paramount importance. There are no more "big, dumb" tackles. All twenty-two men on the field must be using their brains at all times, remembering assignments, listening for signals and trying to outguess and out-judge the opposition in the continual sparring for advantage. The understanding and appreciation of the organization of modern football, its strategy, and the application of the organization and strategy, can provide very real training for fitting young men into similar problems of organization and execution in business, professional and military pursuits.

You, as a spectator, can develop your powers of observation and analysis, your ability to judge psychology and thought processes, and your knowledge of human nature, through close attention to the many facets of a football game. There is sheer entertainment in it as well, and the emotional stimulation of drama, pathos and tragedy such as one can get from attendance at the theater. A healthy point of view will class all these as temporary stimuli. No one should pretend that the winning or losing of one football game is the end of the world, but during the time of attendance the experience can be a very acute one.

Whether it is always admitted or not, football also plays a very important part in the prestige and loyalty an institution can command. Continuing alumni loyalty is all important to the colleges and universities under today's uncertain conditions, and the most immediate bond of common interest, the one most generally brought into conversation, is the football team. A healthy football climate, one that creates respect through the precepts it teaches and the spirit it engenders, not necessarily through the victories it wins, is a tremendous asset to an educational institution.

These remarks have so far all dealt with college football. There is a big public today also interested in the pro game, and you as a spectator will no doubt want to take in this type of play as well. We have spoken of the entertainment value in football, and this is the facet upon which the pros, naturally, focus their attention. They are in business solely to sell tickets to the public and they must keep that public entertained and asking for more.

For that reason, some of the strategic concepts we will outline for you do not enter into the pro game. The coaching picture is also entirely different. Pro players could be called "post-graduates" and should be assumed to know the fundamentals by now. They should also be fairly familiar with the theory and practice of the various offensive systems and should be able to fit into them with less difficulty. Full time can therefore be spent on polishing skills already acquired. The emphasis is always on the spectacular use of these skills for the entertainment of the fans.

Pro football cannot draw on a natural group of undergraduate and alumni supporters, but must create its own "stadium faithful." There will, therefore, be less emphasis on defense, less balance of attack and defense in a sparring contest of strategy, and more wide open action, featuring the forward pass. What the game lacks in refinement of strategy and systems, it makes up for in sheer technique and fast action. In watching the game you may not see many of the elements with which we deal in the following pages and you can concentrate more on mere movement of the ball.

In watching the college game, you will also see, through the increased use and importance of the forward pass, the major influence of the pro sport on the college version. And, remember, by the way, in case you think that your favorite team has the worst pass defense in the country, which seems to be a natural tendency of all fans, that the pros, with all their advanced individual skills, are unable to stop pass completions of some types.

Since football does have so important a place in the American scene today, since it is a game providing so many opportunities for science and refinement, and since a thorough understanding and appreciation of it can only be built on a knowledge of its many elements, let us therefore, see what you, as a spectator, should know about the modern game, starting first with a look into how it is organized. Let's look behind the curtain to the out-of-season months, the weeks of pre-season practice, and the days and nights of a week that leads to the Saturday climax.

II Formations—
Learning the Language

*M*odern football has bred a whole new technical language that perhaps tends to frighten potential devotees away. Before taking you on a tour behind the scenes of the game today and then telling you what to look for on the field of play, it might be a good idea to set your mind at ease on some of this terminology as to formations and positions so that the rest of the discussion will come more easily.

Just as the great number of landlubbers who found themselves running Navy ships in World War II, though they came straight from farms, law offices and college classrooms, discovered that seafaring was not such a great mystery once you learned the language of the old salts, so might viewers of the fascinating human chess game that is modern football find it a lot more comprehensible if they knew in advance what all this special talk is about.

Most of the technical language revolves around the formations used by different coaches to perform the basic intent of the game—moving the ball for a score. A newcomer to football overhearing the talk of a group of coaches or sportswriters might think that there is a bewildering array of these formations, too many for the average spectator to grasp. He would be right in assuming that there are variations on formations ad infinitum, or at least up to the number of coaches teaching the game, but most modern attacks are closely aligned in basic thought. Once their terminology is understood, the variations fall into the picture logically and simply.

First of all, just what is a formation? There are parallels in military strategy, science and business administrations, where definite plans are used to pursue an objective. In football, a formation is the ordered plan for implementing the play of the game. It is limited by the rule which calls for seven or more men on the offensive line of scrimmage, and the choice of a formation and its use are determined by two main factors: personnel available and the inherent capabilities of the coach.

In going into the development of formations, and then the terms that have sprung from them to make up the language of modern football, there is no intention of creating a controversy over their respective merits. That's for you, the fan and spectator, to decide for yourself.

The basic problem behind the need for a formation is a simple one. You have eleven men charged with moving a ball over a defined area against eleven other men. In those early games of the 1860's and 70's all the players pushed and shoved each other and the ball willy-nilly, and the whole thing had all the pattern and science of a greased pig-chase in a cornfield. As in military strategy, where free-for-all club-swinging between cavemen developed into the fantastic complications of modern warfare, the human mind soon saw opportunities for introducing an ordered system into the problem. From that point there has been steady and unending development.

Trial and error over the years have proved the ratio of seven linemen and four backs on offense to be a proper balance, and the rules soon settled on having one man put the ball in play by centering it between his legs instead of having it kicked back. This brought up the problem of orderly reception of the ball in the backfield in order to follow through with the play. The stationing of the man who receives the ball from center is therefore the primary factor in differentiating between the types of offensive formations and often in naming them.

Contrary to what you may believe in listening to modern football terminology, there are fewer formations today than there were in earlier stages of the game's development. Increased press, radio and television coverage has focused greater attention on each individual variation, but there was a time when a team would use a different formation for each play and change the whole business from week to week.

Gradually men of creative thought, the innovators, consolidated order out of this chaos, and through their work we have a well defined group of systems, generally accepted and recognized wherever the game is played.

There were many whose work has been lasting, and among the most influential have been Glenn Warner, Amos Alonzo Stagg, Knute Rockne, Dr. Harry Williams, Fielding Yost, Jock Sutherland, Bernie Bierman, Dick Harlow, Clark Shaughnessy, Ralph Jones, George Halas, Don Faurot and Bud Wilkinson.

These men, by consistent use of a certain formation, developed a whole system around that formation for making all types of plays work. While these systems have become fairly standard, there is nothing against some entirely new ones appearing in the future. The infinite variations possible in moving a ball through the concerted efforts of eleven men are enough to keep coaches' minds working for years to come.

1. Modern Offensive Formations

As we have said, a system and the formation used to implement it, become in detail an individual expression of a coach's own personality, temperament and way of thinking. In general, though, there are only a few major offensive formations. The main ones are: wingback formations, T quarterback formations and punt formations. There is also, of course, a special subdivision for field goals and extra points.

Before we go any further, you should have a graphic picture of these three main definitions. As you can see in Diagram 1, a wingback is an offensive backfield man who lines up just behind the line of scrimmage and just outside his offensive end.

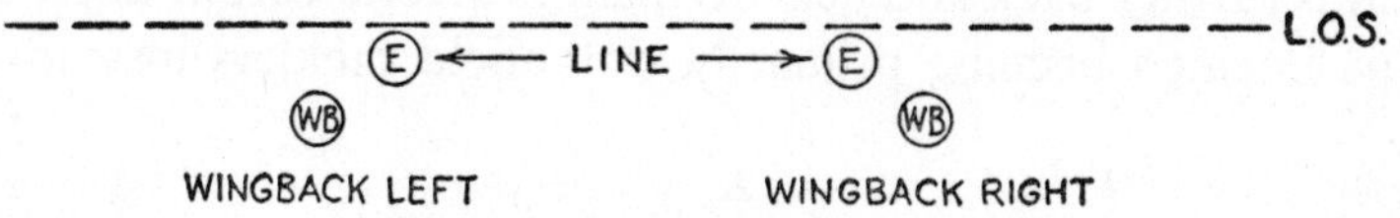

— — — — Ⓔ ⟵ LINE ⟶ Ⓔ — — — — —L.O.S.
⒲ⓑ   ⒲ⓑ
WINGBACK LEFT   WINGBACK RIGHT
Diagram 1—Wingback Position

You may have heard someone refer to a triple wing formation, but that is a misnomer. Since a wingback has to be on the wing of an end and there are only two ends, you can only have single and double wingback formations. When we get to a discussion of flankers, the question of the "third wingback" will be cleared up.

The T Formation gets its name from the basic alignment in which the backfield forms a letter T, with the quarterback directly under center as the stem of the T. There are now many T formations in which this easily discerned "letter line-up" no longer exists, but as long as the quarterback lines up directly back of center to take a handoff instead of receiving the ball with a center pass, these various alignments are still known by some combination of the letter T and modifying terms. Diagram 2, shows a simple T set-up.

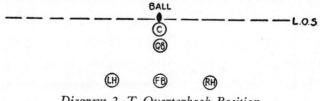

Diagram 2—T Quarterback Position

Diagram 3 shows the spacing of men in a typical Punt Formation. The man who receives the ball on a pass from center is about ten yards back, or more, to give him time and room to get a kick away. Ends are split for ease in getting downfield to cover the kick, and the other backs are lined up for blocking protection of a right footed kicker.

A recent development of the Punt Formation, the Split or Spread Punt Formation, is shown in Diagram 4. The kicker stands further back and gets his main protection from distance. The linemen become primarily downfield tacklers instead of

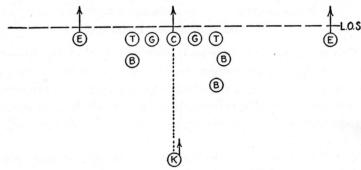

Diagram 3—Punting Formation

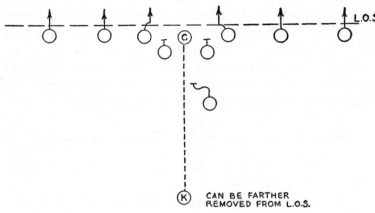

Diagram 4—Spread Punting Formation

protective blockers, holding up just long enough to prevent an unobstructed rush by the defense, while the other backs block against direct rushes on the shortest route over center. The theory is that the five yards or so lost by placing the kicker deep will be more than made up for by preventing punt runbacks by the opposition.

For field goals and extra points, teams line up as in Diagram 5. You may wonder, incidentally, what has happened to the once familiar dropkick in this kind of play. The change of the shape of the ball brought about by the emphasis on passing has made dropkicking a lost art, and the only reasonably sure way of making this kind of kick from the ground, as opposed to a punt in which the foot meets the ball in the air, is to have a man put the ball in place on the ground for the kicker.

USED FOR: 1. POINTS AFTER TOUCHDOWN
2. FIELD GOAL ATTEMPTS

Diagram 5—Placement Kicking Formation

2. LINE DEPLOYMENTS

These are the main basic systems from which all formation terminology stems, but there are many combinations that can be used in them. First of all, the seven men in the line can be deployed in any number of ways. When the word "balance" enters into line deployment, it refers to the odd or even distribution of the linemen on either side of the center over the ball, who is the balance point. Diagram 6 shows a balanced line, and here it might be said that the terms guard, tackle and end for the players in that order away from the center have become so ingrained in football usage that they have remained standard even though they are not always accurately descriptive on offense. Coaches sometimes do away with these terms for simplification purposes while working with their own pupils. The split of the ends away from the tackles has become more or less common for effective operation.

Diagram 6—Balanced Line, Basic Alignment

An unbalanced line, Diagram 7, is commonly one in which there are four men on one side of the center, leaving two on the other. This is exactly the sort of situation where the old designation of guards and tackles breaks down and some coaches use numbers to designate the players. The overbalanced side is called the strong, or, more generally, the long side; and the other side the weak, or short side. We will use long and short from here on. The formation may be long either right or left.

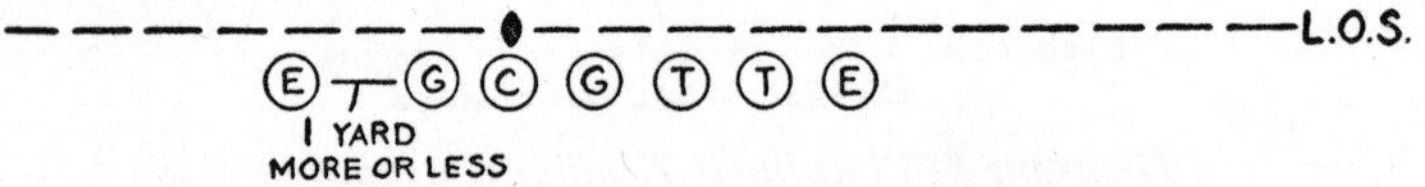

Diagram 7—Unbalanced Line Right, Basic Alignment

Diagram 8 shows a split line, one in which all seven men are separated, or split from the next man, instead of being shoulder to shoulder, in increasing variables according to their distance away from center. The object of this is to spread the strength of the defense by spreading the base of the offense. It almost always uses a balanced line and definite matched splits, as shown in the diagram.

Sounding similar, but meaning something else to a coach, is a line with splits. This could be either a balanced or unbalanced line, with only certain players split from the next man,

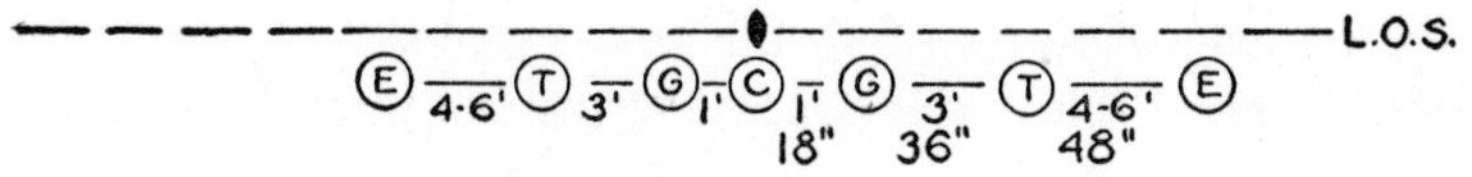

Diagram 8—Balanced Split Line, Basic Alignment

instead of an even pattern; for example, the short side end of an unbalanced line, or the long side end in the absence of a wingback. A line with splits can also mean one in which the guards, tackles and ends are split slightly for blocking room, all at the same distance, instead of in the graduated pattern of a split line.

In Diagram 9 you see a five-one line that is no longer very common since the rules provided for bringing the ball in from the sideline after each play. Do you remember when the center was sometimes an end, crammed against the sideline with the whole formation on one side of him? Then your memory goes back of 1933.

These are the main types of line deployment. The variations are infinite, but we have covered the terms that explain the variations and can now take a look at the backfield deployments.

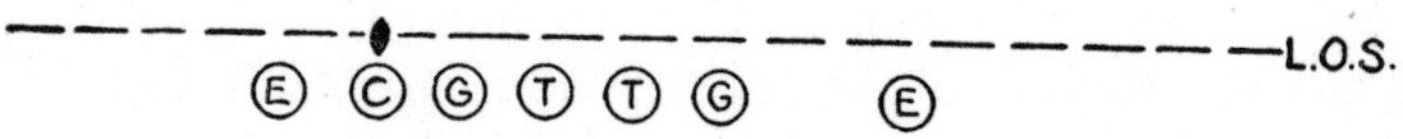

Diagram 9—Five-One Line Alignment

3. BACKFIELD DEPLOYMENTS

Here the individual genius of the coach comes into its most obvious play. The generally accepted formations developed by the "old masters" are used as a base, and the terminology follows from that base, but a coach is only marking time if he has failed to develop some individual backfield deployments. You see them as the plays that are the special property of each team. If all Single Wings or all T Formations were exactly the same, there would be little of suspense, drama or contest in a meeting of teams using the same systems. However, you should get to know the general terms for these basic formations.

Diagram 10 shows a Single Wing deployment with one wingback lined up on the "wing" of the end, in a good blocking position. It also shows the unbalanced line generally used with this deployment, though a balanced line is possible. The quarterback is in an advantageous spot for blocking, and the fullback and tailback are both in a position to receive the center pass.

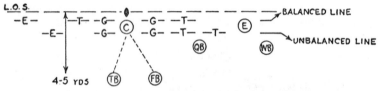

SUPERIMPOSED ON BALANCED AND UNBALANCED LINES

Diagram 10—Single Wing Backfield Alignment

In Diagram 11 we see two types of Double Wing deployments, converting either the fullback or quarterback to a wingback, usually using a balanced line. If the line is balanced the position of the fullback or quarterback in relation to the tailback and center determines whether it is right or left formation.

We have already shown you a T backfield alignment. Here in Diagram 12 is the team lineup of a Straight T, graphically showing how the formation gets its name. Ordinarily the three deep backs are not in such an even line "crossing the T." Usually the fullback is a step behind the halfbacks, and they may take other spacing. Strictly speaking, each of them should be able to receive a direct handoff from the quarterback on a straight ahead movement toward the line.

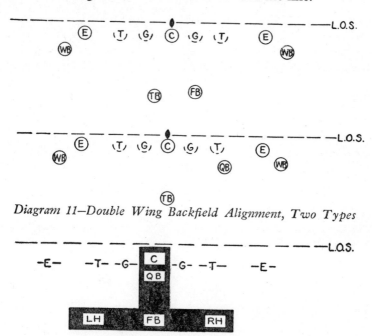

Diagram 11—Double Wing Backfield Alignment, Two Types

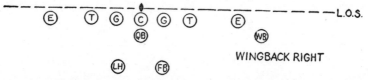

Diagram 12—Basic T Formation Backfield Alignment

When you hear of a Winged T, it means that there is consistent use of both the T-quarterback and wingback-outside-end features in an attempt to gain the advantages of both formations. Diagram 13 shows that the other two backs in a Winged T usually take an alignment similar to the Single Wing deployment.

Diagram 13—Winged T Backfield Alignment

The Box Formation, called the Notre Dame box because it was popularized by the Fighting Irish under Knute Rockne and spread through the football world by the many Rockne players who took up coaching, is an alignment designed to develop out of a shift. The rules slowed the shift with a pause and the formation lost some favor. To the casual observer it may be hard to tell apart from a Single Wing. The backs take up somewhat the same alignment, but they are more closed up. The quarterback is nearer center, and the halfback who is nearer the line of scrimmage is directly behind the split end and therefore not a wingback. The fullback does not stand as close to the tailback. It usually is seen with a balanced line as shown in Diagram 14.

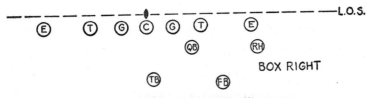

Diagram 14—Box Backfield Alignment

Another formation that the uninitiated might confuse with the Single Wing is the Short Punt, sometimes also called the A Formation, shown in Diagram 15. It is a standard punt formation with the deep man about four yards closer to the center.

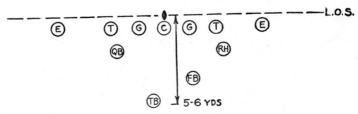

Diagram 15—Short Punt Backfield Alignment

Diagram 16 shows another development of the Punt Formation, the Spread Formation. Both the Short Punt and Spread should lead you to look for a lot of passing. It is in this type of formation that individual coaching genius makes itself most apparent, as it is often sprung as a surprise in order to cross up soundly laid defensive plans or to exploit a good passer playing against an inherently stronger team.

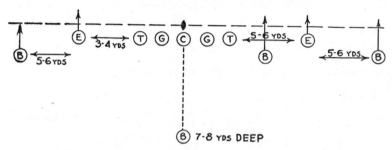

Diagram 16—Typical Spread Backfield Alignment

4. FORMATIONS AFIELD

Now that we have covered the elements that go into making up a formation, the next step is to give some example of how you can expect to see these elements combined and used in systems in operation today. Diagram 17 shows the Single Wing in its two possibilities of balanced and unbalanced line with the standard backfield alignment. There may also be occasional use of other line deployments, such as the five-one, or different splits.

In setting up a five-one line, a coach may bring the short side end over to the long side, or put everybody but the short side end on the long side. This use of linemen-over tends to confuse a defense for a while—until it falls into a pattern. It is therefore only seen occasionally.

In complementing his basic formation with extra variations and maneuvers, a coach today, whether favoring T Formation or Single Wing, probably makes uses of flankers and men in motion. A flanker is simply what his designation implies, a back or end who is lined up wider than the original formation, perhaps achieving a flanking or outside position on the defensive end. He is sometimes erroneously called a third wing-back.

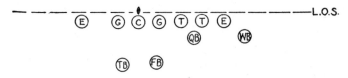

A. SINGLEWING RIGHT, UNBALANCED LINE

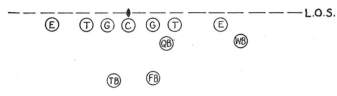

B. SINGLEWING RIGHT, BALANCED LINE

Diagram 17—Single Wings—Backfield and Line Alignments

A man in motion can be a back or end who moves laterally across the field before the ball is snapped. A back must be moving toward his own goal at the moment the ball is snapped, and an in-motion end must be five yards behind the line of scrimmage by then.

There can be any number of flankers but only one man in motion. They both serve the same general purposes: a distraction to the defense, a decoy who must be allowed for and followed in case he is thrown a pass, a potential pass receiver or blocker, and also a means of getting the defense to tip its hand.

In a Single Wing attack, a flanker can be sent to the short side, giving the formation the appearance of a Double Wing, and at the same time a man-in-motion may be used to add to the spread effect. Some Single Wing teams line up in a T and shift to the Single Wing alignment for most plays, while occasionally starting a play direct from the T.

Conversely, the T can go into unbalanced lines and the use of wingback, and may occasionally shift the quarterback out of the spot under center to start a play as a Single Wing maneuver. Diagram 18 shows a Winged T with an unbalanced line, in other words a Single Wing in every respect but the position of the quarterback.

The combination of a straight T backfield alignment and unbalanced line contradicts itself and is seldom seen, but a straight T may end up using a tight line, a split line or a line with splits, as in Diagram 19. The T will also make extensive use of flankers and men-in-motion, perhaps making a wingback out of a flanker as in Diagram 18. Sometimes, when the

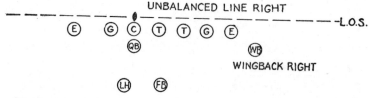

Diagram 18—Winged T Backfield with Unbalanced Line Right

T is using flankers, the quarterback drops back and takes a direct pass from center, especially when the situation very obviously calls for a pass.

Splits in the line can be utilized in the same way to throw a defense off balance.

All these departures from what must be called "normal" formations upset the balance of a formation. Watching what the defense does to combat this change in balance can give a long range idea of what may work and what may not in the course of a game.

For example, a flanker set outside the defensive end for several plays notes that the end is ignoring him. With this in mind, when an opportunity arises in which normal strategy would tend to indicate a play inside end, the offense could

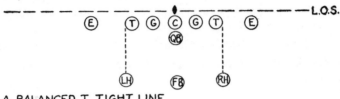

A. BALANCED T, TIGHT LINE

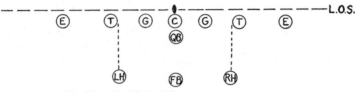

B. BALANCED T, SPLIT LINE

Diagram 19—Tight T and Split T Formations

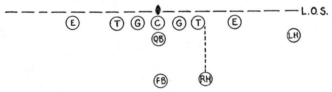

A. BALANCED T, LH FLANKER RIGHT

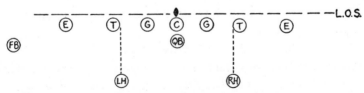

B. BALANCED T, SPLIT, FB FLANKER LEFT

Diagram 20—Tight T and Split T Formations—with Flankers

use an end run or pitchout with the flanker blocking the end in. This should produce a long gainer, and should also have the future effect of having the end play out to the flanker while the defensive halfback behind him comes up fast to cover. This then creates two more possibilities for the offense: running plays inside the end or a forward pass over the halfback who is now coming in fast. And so it goes.

So you can see that there is no such thing as a static formation in modern football. You can also see that the terminology, which may seem bewildering to the uninitiated, is self-defining in many instances. An understanding of how it is arrived at and how it applies can take much of the mystery out of the trade talk of modern football. Equipped with an idea of what all this talk is about, you should now be ready for an exploration behind the scenes of the sport as further background to your role as a Saturday spectator.

III *Long Before the Kick-Off*

*I*t should be realized that much has preceded the appearance of a squad of forty-five or fifty colorfully arrayed players at 2:00 P.M. of a fall Saturday . . . much rehearsing has made possible that choreography of combat spread out below you. This period is a void to many who love the game. Understanding of it should double their interest and enjoyment.

In the first place, those forty-five boys who make up "your squad" are not just plucked at random from the youthful population of your favorite campus. Matriculation does not carry with it a mystic ticket entitling one to a first string spot on the varsity team for that fall. Indeed there are probably no freshmen at all on the varsity squad. All members are either sophomores, juniors or seniors. There are exceptions to the "freshman rule," but the majority of American colleges at present adhere to this policy. It is designed to make it easier for first-year men to adjust to college life without too much pressure and excitement at the very start, and gives them an opportunity to learn the game at the college level against other teams in their own age-bracket. (It is a sensible rule and makes it impossible to abuse the game by bringing in a boy to play football in the fall and then flunking him out at the end of his first semester—which is not just an abuse of the game, but a cruel exploitation of young men.) Anyone on this squad has completed satisfactorily at least one academic year at the institution he represents. But don't write the freshmen out of the varsity picture just because none of them appears with that bright-jerseyed group that races onto the field on game day. And by the same taken, there are others who have made their contribution. What you don't see from your perch above the site of action is just about two-thirds of the organization behind those boys on the field. Let's see how the freshman and junior varsity squads work into the picture of a healthy football situation on any campus.

It goes without saying that a lot of boys like to play football. It also goes without saying that there are individual differences in football ability and experience. Less generally known, perhaps, is the fact that some boys learn and develop more slowly than others. Any coaching staff would be stupid to ignore this group, which has provided some of our best players. It is highly desirable, therefore, to have some sort of a "learning ladder" set up which leads from freshman level football to varsity competition, like the program possible at a fairly large college that is able to carry a freshman, junior varsity, and varsity squad. This will permit the greatest possible number of boys to play the game and insure individual improvement through practice and competition. The problem of how to integrate these three squads is crucial. For better or for worse the emphasis is on performance at the varsity level. How, then, are these three squads, totaling around 135 boys, best organized so that the victories you may logically expect to win during a season will come your way?

1. The Junior Varsity

This squad is made up of players not quite yet ready for varsity competition. Many of its members have shown prom-

ise in the spring and early fall practice sessions, but appear to
need another year of experience. Many boys find it difficult
to make the jump from freshman to varsity competition in one
year. The junior varsity is a way station designed to keep
them active in football and give them a chance to learn and
improve. The size of the jayvee squad will depend primarily
on how it is integrated into the general football picture.

The following problem is a vital one in any football program: In the game as it is played today, your varsity squad
must be prepared to defend itself on any given Saturday against
the machinations of the "T" or the Single Wing formations.
These two or their variations are most generally used today.
Unfortunately for today's defensive strategists, the two formations are widely divergent in their inherent strengths and
weaknesses. Moreover, the fundamentals behind effective use
of either are so different that it is almost impossible to coach a
team to use both. In general, you either use Single Wing or
you use the "T." A synthesis is dangerous and has been
known to be disastrous—for technical reasons which you may
be spared here. It is difficult for a defensive man, trained
against Single Wing, to be prepared to meet a "T" attack—
and vice versa. For this reason most coaches arrange to have
either their jayvee or freshman squads stage that attack which
the varsity does *not* use. But this decision leads to a problem.
Suppose you are a coach teaching Single Wing football at the
varsity level. You want either your jayvee or freshman aggre-
gation to run the T attack against your defense. Which squad
should you have work on this? If they are to handle it effectively, they must work on it all season. It must be *their* attack, to which they are completely committed and on which
they work exclusively, for the better they execute it the better
the varsity defenders will become at solving it.

Working against choice of the jayvees for this season-long
assignment is this factor: These are players who can fit into
the varsity any time their ability merits a promotion. If this

assignment is given them, it makes it almost impossible to move up a jayvee man during the actual season to bolster a position suddenly weakened by injuries. They will be committed to a different offensive system and there simply would not be time enough to teach them the intricacies of the varsity pattern. Perhaps it would be better to have the jayvees use the same system as the varsity. This would permit the carrying of a numerically smaller varsity squad, since the moving up process from junior varsity to varsity would be comparatively simple. Morever, with a smaller varsity squad, the coaching could be more concentrated and effective.

This solution would then force you to carry a freshman squad committed to the T formation. What factors work against this method of providing the varsity with daily rehearsals against the attack the opposition will launch Saturday? If your freshmen run from the T, it means they will complete an entire season without becoming acquainted with the fundamentals of the Single Wing system used by the varsity. Many of the boys coming in as freshmen have been exposed only to the T, which means that preparation for the varsity poses problems of "unlearning" as well as learning. Each year certain boys make the jump directly from freshman to varsity competition without a sojourn on the jayvees. These are often your best prospects, and it would be fruitless to have them come to the varsity coaches completely unacquainted with the system under which they are to play.

The generally accepted formula is, then, for the junior varsity to portray the tactics of the enemy. A somewhat larger varsity squad must be carried and Spring Practice will provide the opportunity for the jayvees to prove their worth and move up to the varsity level. Under this arrangement, the freshman will be free to concentrate on the fundamental skills and techniques that are the foundations on which varsity performance rests.

The junior varsity, then, will be an important factor in any success that may come to the varsity during the year. It is important to have the jayvees near by during the fall—on adjacent fields if possible—so that no time is lost in bringing the two squads together. Under the platoon conditions of the past few years, both offensive and defensive segments of the jayvees could be worked against the varsity at the same time. Under the new and sharp limitations upon substitutions, the time element becomes even more vital as each player must now try to learn approximately twice as many details and techniques. It is upon these reserves that the offensive and defensive tools of the varsity are honed during the week. And there is no rest for the weary. Often the junior varsity is used on Monday to scrimmage, under full game conditions, the varsity substitutes who did not see much action in the varsity game on Saturday. Of course, the jayvees may well have played a game of their own that day, too—but for them, no rest! They go right back to tough contact work against the varsity subs who are eager to rate starting berths and look upon Monday's battle with the jayvees as the best spot to catch the coach's eye. This Monday struggle is often tougher physically on the junior varsity players than their Saturday games.

On Tuesdays, Wednesdays and Thursdays, the jayvees impersonate the attack and defensive maneuvers of next Saturday's opponent. Friday brings their lone chance to try to assemble their own attack for their game next day; the lack of time generally dictates that their repertoire will be a hodgepodge of the varsity's opponents' favorite plays. In their huddle the quarterback will often call the play by the name of teams the varsity has met during the season: "The Army Trap"; "The Illinois Pitchout"; "The Virginia Split T End Run"; "The Notre Dame Pass." The jayvees are simply so busy adjusting their basic formation to resemble the attack of most of the varsity opponents that they have no time for an organized signal-calling system of their own. They must learn quickly. Nothing they do can be really polished and this in itself is often discouraging.

There are compensations, however. Their contests are played before the varsity games at most colleges, so they are free to watch the "main show" on Saturday afternoon. Here they have real enjoyment, for they are in the best possible position to appreciate what is going on below. Not only do they recognize the opponents' personnel, but they can fully appreciate the plays they use. A junior varsity back who has been impersonating all week one of the opponents' stars—often even wearing his number—will watch that player with great interest. Most of the maneuvers will be familiar to him. He will be able to see how the player whose role he took fares against the defenses that have been set up to stop him. A smart jayvee would be an excellent companion at a big game, for he knows all the defensive and offensive game plans. After all, he has worked against the varsity for many hours during the past week and has seen these plans develop. He should know their strong and weak spots, be familiar with who is hurt, who is weak in certain departments of the game, who will be featured in the attack and a thousand and one other details that have been unfolded before him during the week, including any special plays that have been designed for that particular occasion. Indeed the jayvee, working constantly against varsity offensive and defensive units, has an unusual opportunity to gain a thorough grounding in football strategy and tactics. His week is a rough one, but his own games and those of the varsity's that he sees, go a long way toward repaying him for all that he contributes to his college's football program. Always ahead—and often realized before his college career ends—is the goal of elevation to a place on the varsity squad. Many top flight teams owe a measurable portion of their success to the all-around ability of a senior who learned the hard way— a season or two in the thick of scrimmaging for the jayvees.

2. The Freshman Squad

Fall of freshman year launches the basic football program through which every candidate must go. It is here that the fundamentals of the formation used by the varsity are taught at the most elementary level. Usually the turn-out for freshman football is heavy. For a variety of reasons, any boy just entering college will normally report for freshman football if he has had any previous experience whatsoever.

Freshman football is one of the first group projects open to the entering class and presents a fine opportunity to meet and know many of one's classmates. Moreover, it is a boy's first chance to earn recognition and prestige within his class. This holds true too, of course, for the other fall freshman sports, but football draws the lion's share, often attracting well over one hundred boys for the first practice sessions. This presents a coaching problem that is generally solved by a rigorous conditioning program in which the first few days serve to weed out those who are not serious contenders prepared to work and work hard. At the same time, a freshman coaching staff must be able to recognize potential ability early, for it is essential to cut an unwieldy squad to a workable group of forty-five or fifty with all possible speed.

Once the freshmen have been shaken down to these specifications, the real teaching program begins. These boys have played many different types of football on varying levels of competition and some will have to "unlearn" habits and techniques they may have used for years. Progress can be slow and discouraging until players and coaches become well acquainted. A freshman team seldom looks like a polished and cohesive whole. Its attack will be similar to the varsity's but, of course, the execution will be on a much lower level. Moreover, the offense is generally sharply limited in an effort to make sure that what the freshmen do learn, they learn well.

Whenever the varsity is preparing to face teams with offensive formations similar to its own, the freshmen are used to simulate the opponent's attack in much the same fashion that the jayvee squad does in other weeks.

Some colleges believe that it is not important for the freshmen to play outside games. They feel that there is so much to learn that the need for preparation to meet other teams merely limits the freshman coaches in the amount of time they can devote to teaching. The majority agree, however, that outside competition is important at the freshman level. Experience thus gained is considered vital in developing poise and the ability to perform under game conditions. Moreover, it gives the player a sense of anticipation and adds meaning to the fundamental lessons of the weekly practice. Outside games contribute much to squad morale and keep the players working hard to improve themselves.

It is axiomatic that some freshmen will develop more quickly than others, but it is vital not to lose sight of the boy with promise whose development may come a bit later. In the final analysis, this is the real reason for the freshman-jayvee-varsity hierarchy. The junior varsity is the intermediate level in the development of top flight football players. Some players will skip this step, but they are not necessarily the best performers in the long run. Few sophomores break into the starting line-up and by junior and senior year the boy who spent his sophomore year as a jayvee may be ready to move up. He has been playing ball at the junior varsity level while his classmate has been "riding the bench" on the varsity. The slower developing boy, instead of becoming discouraged and giving up football, has thus had a chance to work and play his way into varsity competition. By his senior year, he may be a better football player than his teammate who did not have to come up the hard way.

3. THE COACHING STAFF

The organization of any staff depends primarily upon the theories and practices of the head coach, and there is accordingly considerable variation in staff duties and responsibilities throughout the country. Certain factors, however, are rather widely accepted, primarily among them the policy that the head coach selects his own staff whose members are then responsible to him.

Coaching staffs are in a peculiarly vulnerable position. Every Saturday during the season, their handiwork is exposed in sharp competition with that of their competitors. Moreover, that competition is viewed by thousands whose reactions have been known to be "packaged in prejudice and wrapped with intolerance." The head coach hears early and often about his team's mistakes and shortcomings. That many of these criticisms are neither correct nor charitable does little to lessen the cumulative effect of the mailman's visits. A coaching staff must be prepared to hang together, not separately. If a staff's sense of proportion and humor can survive a "long season," it is fortunate indeed. At any rate, its members must have complete confidence in each other's loyalty and friendship.

In the past, as a result of the trend toward platoon football, a head coach generally sought to assemble a staff composed of a backfield coach, a line coach, an end coach, and a defensive coach. Many varsity staffs, of course, were smaller than this, depending on the size of the college, but a five-man staff was a fair example of the pattern in platoon coaching. The line, end and backfield coaches are traditional. Their duties lie mainly in the sphere of the game which their titles indicate, with the accent on offense.

The defensive coach has been a newcomer on the scene—having arrived simultaneously with the advent of platoons. His duties have involved, almost entirely, coordination of the defensive efforts of linemen, ends and backs. He was assisted at various times by all the other coaches, depending on where coaching emphasis was needed. He was responsible, among other things, for the defensive efforts against a passing attack, for coordinating linebackers with the line against a running game, for working with ends and halfbacks to stop sweeps. It is not intended here to speak of the defensive coach in the past tense simply because of the revolutionary rule changes which have eliminated two-platoon football. It may well be that coaching techniques learned under two-platoon conditions will carry over into one-platoon football and raise the level of coaching high above what it was in the days before World War II. It is becoming increasingly clear that the defensive coach is here to stay. It will be interesting to see over the next few seasons just how he is integrated into the football plans of various institutions.

Defense today actually has many advantages over the offense. It is not required to play a certain number of men on the line of scrimmage. The defense can play eleven men on the line—or no men at all, while the offense must at all times have at least seven men there. The offensive men on the line of scrimmage must be motionless for a full second before the ball is snapped—not so the defense. Their men, on or off the line, can be moving all over the place. With this advantage, the defense has a wide range of devices it can use to confuse and frustrate the offense. In recent years defensive platoons have been meeting the offensive with plays of their own—team maneuvers in which every man has specific duties and responsibilities. All this must be taught, rehearsed, and practiced under pressure. The defensive coach oversees all this, directs his men against the junior varsity attacking units, and constantly strives for all-around improvement.

The well-rounded staff will also have a freshman coach and a junior varsity coach. The freshman coach, whose assistants are likely to vary from year to year, must understand the fundamentals of line, backfield and end play as taught offensively and defensively at the varsity level—to enable him to direct the labors of his own semi-volunteer staff. The junior varsity coach, working with the varsity every day, must integrate his own practice program with theirs almost on a minute-by-minute basis.

All these men should have played and loved the game themselves, although it is not by any means necessary that they should have been great players. The important thing is that they be able to interpret to their players the many and increasingly complex details of modern football. They themselves must be students of the game, as it is constantly changing and developing. It is no longer enough for some former All-American to say, "Do it the way I used to do it." Often the boy hasn't, nor never will have, the ability to do it that way. Increasingly today a "way" must be found for the boy—not a boy for the "way." The premium in coaching is on patience, study and teaching ability. This will be increasingly true under the present trend toward greater faculty supervision and elimination of flagrant recruiting practices.

An important part of the football organization that seldom receives recognition is the medical department. This generally consists of the team physician and, under his supervision, a corps of trainers who vary in number according to the institution served. The trainers take care of all minor injuries to varsity, jayvee and freshman squads and supervise all equipment problems. These are the men whose educated hands "work out" the bruises and stiffness that every football player accepts as part of the game. Many of these men put a lifetime of service into their jobs. Their experience and their close acquaintance with the players often make them the morale builders of the squad in a very real way. They make certain, through a million and one services, that "their boys" are ready physically and psychologically for the big game on Saturday. Under the direction of the team physician, they spend many hours with an injured boy helping him through the use of graded exercises, massage, protective taping, and various other types of treatment.

Experience shows that ninety-five per cent of all football injuries can be traced to three sources: poor equipment; lack of physical conditioning; and poor teaching techniques. The remaining five percent of the injuries are simply due to the natural hazards of a physical contact game. These three main causes are constantly under attack by doctors, trainers, and coaches who know that nothing wrecks a football program more surely than untimely and unnecessary injuries. New equipment is constantly being tested in an effort to assure better protection for the players. Top flight physical condition is sought from the first day of practice through a variety of drills and routines, and daily practice sessions are carefully planned to eliminate injuries. Excessive contact in any one session is barred. Boys are thoroughly "warmed up" before being exposed to full-scale scrimmage conditions and are not permitted to become too tired before being withdrawn. Once good condition is attained, the problem is primarily one of keeping the players "sharp." Too much scrimmaging is carefully avoided in an effort to reduce further the five per cent injury toll.

A constant effort, of course, is made to better a boy's technique in blocking and tackling. Today most coaches scrimmage by "parts" only—that is, they may work on end runs against only a defensive end, a defensive linebacker and a defensive halfback. This is done to cut down the chances of injury due to piling on or "gang tackling" which would be bound to take place with eight other defensive men in the picture. Moreover, this concentration on the key blocks allows the coaches to do a much better job of teaching the techniques which, by their very effectiveness, rule out the awkwardness that leads to injury. By these means, then, a great deal has been done to reduce the incidence of serious football injuries. Bruises and strains are bound to be a part of the game—but after all, the subway at rush hour has not solved this problem either!

4. Pre-Season Planning

It is small exaggeration to say that pre-season preparation starts with the whistle ending the final game. Throughout the winter, motion pictures of the past season's action are run tirelessly over and over, providing a great deal of data for thought and study. During the season, the films have been used primarily to teach the players, but during the winter they are used to teach the coaches. Each player has been graded on every offensive and defensive play in which he has participated, his mistakes have been pointed out and every effort is made to correct them. The major emphasis during the season has been on a study of personnel—an effort to have the best man for each position actually playing in that spot.

During the winter, the plays themselves are studied, play analyses are drawn up for the whole season and examined. For instance, it is important to determine precisely what success certain plays have achieved under certain conditions. If the off-tackle play is under discussion, it is important to know just what it has accomplished. What has been its average gain over the season? What defensive man has most often stopped it? What has it gained against certain types of defense? What has it done when flankers are set out? What have been the results when run to the wide side of the field—to the closed, or near side of the field? Has it proved itself in the zone of most intense resistance, when the team is driving for a score from the opponents' ten yard line? Has it gained more when run on an early down with long yardage to go, or has it proved better on a late down with short yardage? Many coaches, in studying their attacks, want to know what a play has done on first down and ten yards to go; second down and over five; second and under five; third and over five; third and under five; and fourth down with any yardage. This sort of study can, of course, be carried still further and is undertaken by most coaches in some form or other for every running and pass play in their repertoire.

At the same time, a good deal of thought goes into an examination of offensive and defense strategy of opponents. Do they like to use certain types of defense against passing or for plays when big yardage is at stake? Do their defenses over the years begin to fall into any kind of pattern which will allow you to guess something of their defensive plans for the season ahead?

Coaches also study their opponents' plays to build better defenses against them. Defensive lapses are scrutinized and the type of play that produced the breakdown is examined. Then, too, the quarterbacking strategy of the opponents is watched closely. When do they like to pass? From what position on the field are their most successful passes thrown? Sometimes all running plays and passes of an opponent over a couple of years are charted on a field pattern, with down and distance noted. This will often fall into a recognizable pattern and provide valuable tips for your next season's defensive plans against that particular team. All this means many hours gathering the data from the game pictures and then more hours studying it and breaking it down into ideas for the future.

Many of the ideas that are gleaned from game movies over the winter are put to the test in Spring Practice, the "laboratory" for modern football. Play series that appear sound on the blackboard by the light of the winter sun often wither and die outdoors in the bright spring sunshine. This is the time for experimentation, both with ideas and with men. The halfback who did not quite make the team the previous fall may find himself an end. A fullback who has had trouble handling the ball may be just the man for a guard position. Indeed the fine Army lines of the Blanchard-Davis era at West Point were largely made up of backs whom Blanchard and Davis had relegated to the bench, a factor that gave the Army lines of those years tremendous speed and mobility.

The time to make these switches in position is during Spring Practice, when there is plenty of time to work on fundamentals without the problem of readying the squad for a new opponent each Saturday. Spring Practice provides the opportunity to make personnel decisions that will determine what players are to be invited back to early fall practice. Without the spring period, it is difficult for a staff to equate the abilities of a jayvee of the past fall with an up and coming freshman. Has the added year of experience for the jayvee more than made up for the greater innate ability with which the freshman may be blessed? The freshman coaches recommend players to the varsity staff, as do the junior varsity coaches. Without the Spring Practice period, it is impossible to evaluate their relative abilities, since they have not previously really competed against each other for positions. Experience is still one of our best teachers and the opportunity to play the game in the spring is vital to the learning process in modern football.

Some colleges have overdone Spring Practice, both in the time devoted to it and in their demands for compulsory attendance. Sensibly limited as to time, and without compulsion for those who are engaged in other spring sports, it should contribute a great deal to the overall health of the football program. As long as players are able to work their way from freshman year to the junior varsity and finally the varsity, the total picture will be one of enthusiasm and sacrifice among the players. No one wants to stay a jayvee forever. Nothing helps the morale of that squad so much as to see its erstwhile members playing on the varsity; and remember that the morale of the jayvees is an important factor, since these are the men who furnish a great deal of the day-to-day competition for the varsity team.

Spring Practice is normally climaxed by an inter-squad game or games, of which motion pictures are taken so that the coaches can study the personnel under "combat conditions." The coaching staff decides, usually by the end of June, who will be invited back for the early fall practice sessions. During the summer they keep in touch with the squad by sending each member a critique of his Spring Practice work and an analysis, taken from the films, of his play in the spring game.

Often it is hoped that the players will do some sort of conditioning work at a leisurely pace through the summer, and the kickers and passers generally are given a ball for working on their specialties at home. All are urged to do some running and calisthenics in the latter part of August so that they report in early September in some semblance of condition. Many men look for a tough, out-door type of summer work in an effort to strengthen themselves, and they are the best prepared when the early September workouts begin.

"Back to the Salt Mines!" Pre-season practice in the fall varies to some extent but essentially it merits the football players' description as "the salt mines." Some colleges conduct practice on their own campuses while others establish a football camp in some secluded spot a number of miles away. This latter procedure is often preferable, since it gets the players away by themselves where there are no distractions and where they can concentrate on football and football alone. Moreover, the camp life, bringing everyone together on the same level, tends to break down any inter-class barriers that may exist, and it sets the foundation for solid squad morale.

These are the days of double workouts in a period generally lasting about two weeks before classes begin. It is literally true that in this period the season is often made or lost. These two weeks, because of the double workouts, the longer sessions, the fact that each week is good for six days instead of a scant four (as in the regular season, when nothing is done on

Fridays before a game and very little on Mondays after a game) are of great importance. They are worth six weeks anywhere else in the fall program.

Here is the way a typical day at football camp might be scheduled in the early part of September:

6:45—Rise and Shine
7:00-7:05—Breakfast (doors locked at 7:05. Late comers tighten belts!)
8:45-10:45—Practice
11:00—Swimming if desired—but make it short!
11:15—Dinner
12:00-3:30—Recreation (Sleep suggested, urged and advised.)
3:30—Meetings with Coaches
4:15—Lunch
5:30—Specialists report (Kickers and Passers)
5:45-7:45—Practice
8:30—Sandwiches and fruit juices
8:45-9:30—Meetings with Coaches
10:00—Lights Out.

This program, of course, has as many variations as there are colleges engaging in these early season workouts, but the general pattern holds pretty well at all camps. The principal aim is to complete two good daily workouts of about two hours apiece. This is hard physical work and, in order to get the most out of the squad, it is important to avoid practicing during the hottest part of the day. There is always an attempt to insure a period of sleep and rest before each session on the field. Some coaching staffs work even earlier in the morning and hold their second workout just as late in the day as the light will allow. Between times, there are meetings with the coaches at which the mistakes of the session just concluded can be gone over, or the problems of the coming practice discussed. This is generally done at mid-day, while in the evening there is sufficient time to study the ever informative movies. It is a full day, with the work poured on, and the boys seldom complain when the curfew rings at 10:00 P.M.

5. COACHING TECHNIQUES AND PROCEDURES

Football is a mass of detail well learned and efficiently executed. Given any degree of equality as to personnel, competition among coaches today is to obtain the best teaching techniques and apply them most intelligently. Agreement as to what constitutes good running, passing, blocking and tackling is almost unanimous among coaches today but in the sphere of how to teach these skills, agreement is practically non-existent. Every coach has his own pet drills and favorite exercises designed to teach the fundamentals of the game. When the discussion moves into the field of team maneuvers, such as pass defense or the deep reverse, the debate as to teaching methods waxes well nigh homicidal.

Because of the widespread use of motion pictures, there are few secrets left in designing formations or creating plays. The deciding factors in any fairly even game today lie in the manner that each team executes its plays and reduces the number of mistakes it makes. Coaching techniques are the methods used *on the practice field* to teach the boys as quickly and efficiently as possible the many skills and details of modern football. These methods vary so widely and are so technical in many of their aspects that detailed examination of them would be out of place in a book designed for the average football fan.

It should, however, be of interest to show a typical practice schedule for a Wednesday in the midst of a busy season. The time element, as stressed earlier, is so important today that the ability of a coaching staff to utilize its hours on the practice field is often decisive. There is so much material to be covered that every minute of practice time must be used to the best advantage. All mistakes of the previous week must be corrected in both individual and team play and weaknesses must be strengthened on the same basis.

Some of the individual work can be done early, before the entire squad is dressed and ready. Because arrival time for all the squad will often vary depending on late classes or taping and equipment problems, the specialists will generally get their assignments first. Kickers and passers often receive personal attention before anyone else is on the field. Then "group work" will start: linemen, ends and backs reporting to their respective coaches. Here work on technique and detail is not hindered because one or two players may still be absent. Individual attention is given to each man and problems are worked out so that when practice for the team as a unit starts there will be a minimum of mistakes and confusion.

When the last squad member is on the field, work starts on a team basis. In two platoon days, perhaps the first string defensive group would test its defenses for next Saturday against jayvees, using the opponent's offense, while the "A" offensive team improved its downfield blocking on plays run outside the ends. The "B" offensive group perhaps would work on protecting the passer against the "B" defensive group. There must be rotation so that all players are given some work in each department. Later, attention would be paid to the kicking game; to the blocking or running back of punts for the defense and to protecting and covering punts for the offense. The 1953 rule changes altered details of how such a program is run, but the main object of keeping all candidates busy cannot be changed—actually every minute becomes doubly important for the players now must learn all details of both offense and defense. This puts a further premium on good teaching and efficient use of the time available for practice sessions. If the "A" eleven is working on offense with the offensive coaches it is now doubly important that the "B" eleven be working with the defensive coaches. Not a moment can be wasted if the present high level of play in college football is to be maintained.

IV Choosing Personnel

*J*ust what are the coaches looking for in the candidates for the various positions on today's teams? How do they settle on a lineup from all that raw material on the hoof? First, let's take the backfield positions. The names of these are sometimes a bit confusing, as they came originally from British rugby and referred to the distance behind the scrimmage line that each man played. Today, halfbacks, fullbacks and quarterbacks are pretty well mixed up in the various formations used. In the straight T, which is the oldest of American formations, the backfield alignment comes closest to the original British. To refresh your memory, it looks like this:

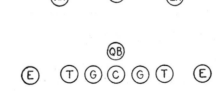

Diagram 21—Normal T Formation Alignment

The quarterback has his hands under the center to receive the ball (originally it used to be kicked back to him) and the full-back is the deepest of the backs, being the middle man of the three deep men. The halfbacks—right half and left half—are on either side and are about even with the fullback, though sometimes a bit nearer the line of scrimmage. In the Single Wing formation, the positions are a bit different, if you remember:

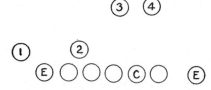

Diagram 22—Normal Single Wing Alignment

Here, numbers 1 and 4 are the halfbacks, number 3 is the fullback and number 2 is the quarterback. Because of the positions of the halfbacks, number 1 is now referred to as the wingback and number 4 is called the tailback. A halfback, years ago, was moved over to a wingback position in order to flank the defensive tackle—he is on the end or wing of the formation and is a yard back from the offensive line—therefore, the name wingback. The other halfback is, in a sense, at the tail end of the formation, the farthest man back, hence the tail-back.

Let's look again for a moment at the two formations, the two basic alignments from which modern football launches its attack. Looking at the T, you see a formation that is completely balanced in relation to the position of the ball. The T can strike with the same rapidity straight ahead or around either end. The simplest and most basic play from this formation occurs when the quarterback accepting the ball from the center, simply pivots and hands it to either halfback driving straight ahead. Known in the trade as the "handoff" or "dive" play, this is the fastest hitting play in football and every defense must stop it or be cut to ribbons.

Looking further at the formation, it is apparent that the T quarterback will do almost all the ball handling. His position alone will preclude the possibility of a direct pass from the center to any other man in the backfield. This direct pass can be effected through the quarterback's legs, but it is not used to any great extent by most T coaches. The other backs must learn to accept the ball effectively from the quarterback, but they do not have primary ball handling responsibility in the T backfield.

Now glance for a moment at the Single Wing. Here is a formation that is completely unbalanced in relation to the position of the ball. Not only is the line unbalanced, with four men on one side of the ball and two on the other, but the backs are very definitely overbalanced toward the "long side" of the line. It should be apparent that the Single Wing cannot hit with equal power and speed to both sides. It is, on the other hand, gauged to deliver its most potent blow at the defensive tackle who plays in the vicinity of the "long side" offensive end. The off-tackle play—run to the strong side of the formation—is to the Single Wing what the "handoff" is to the T. It is the most powerful play from Single Wing formation and the one that all intelligently planned defenses must be prepared to stop. They are so prepared, you may be sure. Few T teams run wild with their "handoffs" today, nor do many Single Wing teams crush the defenders with the famous Pittsburgh off-tackle drives of Jock Sutherland's day. The defenses have caught up and these plays today must be run with flankers, splits and other technical devices designed to offset the maneuvers of the defense. They are still, however, the basic threats of both formations.

It should be apparent from a glance at game action that the quarterback requirements in the two formations are as different as day and night, as sharp in contrast as the motions of a

POINT AFTER TOUCHDOWN—"THE MOST IMPORTANT PLAY OF THE GAME"

NOTRE DAME VS. OKLAHOMA

United Press-Acme News Pictures

RETURNING THE KICKOFF
PRINCETON VS. PENNSYLVANIA
Photo by Alan Richards

DRIVING FOR EXTRA YARDS
MISSOURI VS. CALIFORNIA
United Press-Acme News Pictures

SCORING AROUND THE END
YALE vs. PRINCETON
Photo by Alan Richards

THE LAST WHITE LINE
ARMY VS. NAVY
United Press-Acme News Pictures

FOR THE FIRST DOWN
PRINCETON VS. CORNELL
Acme Pictures

PERFECT CONTROL
PRINCETON VS. YALE
Wide World Photo

THE PERFECT INITIAL OPENING

NOTRE DAME VS. NORTH CAROLINA

United Press-Acme News Pictures

THE END ZONE COMPLETION
PRINCETON VS. PENNSYLVANIA
Photo by Alan Richards

STOPPED BY THE END AND LINEBACKER

PURDUE VS. MICHIGAN STATE

United Press-Acme News Pictures

THE END ZONE VIEW

U.S.C. VS. STANFORD

United Press-Acme News Pictures

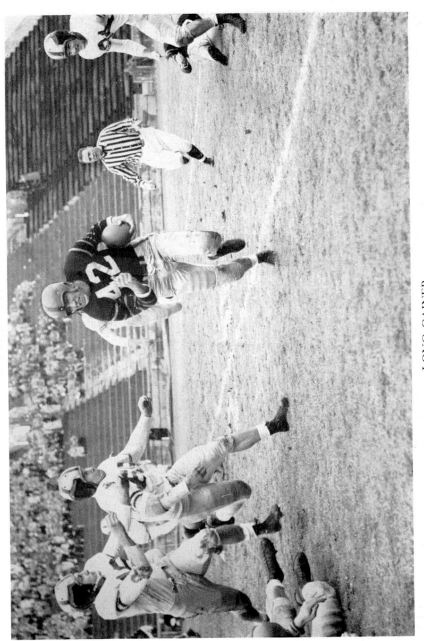

LONG GAINER

DARTMOUTH VS. PRINCETON

Princeton Alumni Weekly

ACTION IN THE ROSE BOWL

U.S.C. VS. WISCONSIN

United Press-Acme News Pictures

RUSHING THE PASSER

PRINCETON VS. HARVARD

Photo by Alan Richards

THE BLOCKERS PAVE THE WAY

MICHIGAN VS. NORTHWESTERN

United Press-Acme News Pictures

THE PERFECT PASS

PRINCETON VS. PENNSYLVANIA

Life

ballerina and a truck driver. The T quarterback is a ball
handler, a passer, and a faker; the Single Wing Quarterback is
a blocker, first and last. The man in the T does not have to be
a ball carrier of any great ability—he is too close to the line to
pick up any momentum to plunge through it and, in order to
circle the ends, would first have to run backward. Yet he
must be a constant threat at all times. This he achieves by
his passing, at which he *must* be adept. Danger must always
exist that at the conclusion of his ball-handling and faking,
the quarterback will straighten up and throw a perfect pass
for a long gain. He should enjoy fooling people, for the deception of the T depends on him. Indeed, he is relieved of all
blocking chores to make sure that he can concentrate on this
deception.

For the Single Wing quarterback, however, glamour is out.
As indicated above, his chores deal with blocking and little
else. No legerdemain for him as he blocks ends, traps tackles,
and cuts down linebackers. He and a T quarterback won't
even look like the same breed. The T quarter might well be
tall and slender, for height is an advantage that enables him to
see over his blockers to pick out his receivers downfield. The
Single Wing field general might well be built close to the
ground, stocky and rugged to withstand the battering he must
take in his blocking assignments. Both boys, however, must
be smart, as they direct their teams on the field. They should
be leaders and highly respected by their teammates, since the
decisions they must make and the reactions to them of the
other ten players, are decisive factors in the game.

In filling the halfback positions, speed is the keynote. There
is simply no substitute for speed, especially for ball carrying
and in both formations halfbacks "carry the mail." The duties
of the T halfbacks are identical. Because the formation is perfectly balanced, the assignments of the right halfback are a
"mirror vision" of those of the left half. Of course, over the

span of a season a right half becomes accustomed to moving to his right, and a left half to his left, making it difficult to switch positions at will, although it has been done. In the Single Wing, on the other hand, there is no similarity whatsoever between the assignments of a wingback and a tailback.

For T halfbacks, requirements are speed and ball-carrying ability. On the rapidity with which they can reach the line of scrimmage hangs much of the split-second timing that makes their offense roll. These halfbacks do not have to be ballhandlers in any sense other than in expert ability to accept the ball from the quarterback, nor do they have to be passers, although it helps if they can throw the running pass either to the right or left. They must, however, be able to fake and fake well. Their position five yards back of the line of scrimmage limits their blocking to ends and linebackers—a type of openfield blocking. Actually they fake more than they block —primarily because of the position in which they line up at the start of the play.

Single Wing halfbacks must be considered one at a time, as the requirements for each position are so different. The tailback *must* be a passer—there can be no compromise here! If he can't pass, he must play somewhere else. He should also be a runner of better than average ability, but does not have to be a blocker. He will accomplish more by faking than by blocking, in any event, since his running and passing are such a threat at all times. In this, he is like the T quarterback. Ball-handling ability is important, too, as the tailback receives the ball on a direct pass from the center and must initiate many of the offensive maneuvers in the Single Wing backfield. Ideally a triple threat back should play at this position, as it helps to have the threat of a kick here, too. However, in this age of specialists one seldom finds the three talents combined adequately in one individual. The passing and running are absolutely essential—the kicking is the frosting on the cake.

The wingback should be the fastest of the backs, since he must run the reverses—the plays directed back to the "short side" of the formation—and thus has the longest distance to go before he reaches the hole. Unlike the tailback, he must be a blocker and a good one. His double team block with the long side end on the defensive tackle is the key to Single Wing's basic off-tackle play. In addition he should be the best pass catcher among the backs, because his position out on the flank and close to the scrimmage line makes it possible for him to get downfield in a hurry.

Fullbacks in both formations are normally chosen as power runners who can drive into the line with real impact. They serve to keep defensive alignments closed up, thus giving the halfbacks a chance to sparkle on their outside running. Both formations ask their fullbacks to block ends on wide sweeps by the halfbacks. It is not necessary to have a passer at this spot, although if he happens to possess talent in this department it can be utilized.

Studying the Single Wing formation a bit further, you will note that the fullback is in a position to receive direct passes from the center. This means that the player must be a ball handler here to a greater extent than if he were part of the T. Indeed, if Single Wing stresses the "spin series" by the fullback, it will be necessary for this man to be a top-flight ball handler and faker. In this series, the ball handling and deception are in the hands of the fullback. He needs to be as clever in this department as the T quarterback, while still executing ball carrying and blocking chores. The T fullback is not as complicated a position to play as is the same spot in Single Wing.

Under the rule changes doing away with two platoon specialists, assignment of the offensive backs to their most effective defensive post should take in the following considerations. Speed and inherent ball-handling ability in pass defense are most important. This latter can only be taught to a certain extent. Beyond that it is an instinct.

The safety man should be the best pass defender and must be very fast in order to cover the maximum amount of ground. It will help if he is tall—many quarterbacks' mouths will water at the sight of a short safety man. They promptly send their tall receivers downfield, hurl the pigskin high in the air, and gleefully abide by the results of a basketball jump for possession between a 5'9" safety man and a 6'3" end. Tackling ability is a requisite, although it is not as important as pass defense or ability to handle kicks surely. The safety man should be the most experienced of the three deep backs in the normal defensive alignment, for he is the final barrier between your opponents and your goal line. If he makes a serious mistake, it will be a sure touchdown for the opposition. His judgment on when to handle punts and when to leave them alone is vital. Many a game has been lost by an inexperienced safety man's error in attempting to handle a kick in a crowd. With your coolest, most experienced, and best pass-defending back at safety position, you will be able to relax on the bench—or in the stands—with some degree of confidence that complete disaster will not strike.

At the defensive halfbacks, one should look for good tacklers first and then for good pass defenders. The left defensive halfback is generally your best tackler, since most teams run better to their right. Again, speed is important, for it will allow a defensive man to make a wrong move and still catch up on the play.

Linebackers are chosen primarily for their ability to tackle. Theirs is the roughest spot on the field, because they are expected to make the lion's share of the tackles and must meet the ball carriers head on at the line of scrimmage. Here impact is at a maximum, since there is normally little room for the ball carrier to dodge at the scrimmage line. For this reason linebackers must be rugged, durable characters. Every effort is made by the offensive team to block them with linemen and backs, who chop at them from every angle, and the linebacker should have heavy underpinnings in order to shake off these blocks. Speed is not the first requirement for this position, though it is always important. Ability to diagnose plays quickly and move to the scene of action are the qualities sought in a linebacker. These men are generally born, not made—much as hitters are in baseball. They must have a fundamental love of contact which places them always in the middle of the play. Pass defense has grown increasingly important for them and it is here that the need for speed is felt, although it remains secondary to ability to tackle well and shed blockers without being knocked down.

In single platoon football, the most probable position for the T quarterback is the safety position where his defensive duties will be least arduous. He is much too valuable an offensive cog to be exposed to the battering of a linebacker's spot, or faced with the constant necessity of tackling against outside plays from the defensive halfback position. No doubt the fullback, being the most robust of the backs, will handle the linebacker's chores on defense and the two halfbacks will handle their defensive posts as best they can. You may find a Single Wing offensive backfield swinging to defense a bit differently. The quarterback, a different "breed of cat" from the T quarterback, may well handle a defensive halfback position. No doubt the fullback will back up the line as will his T counterpart. The tailback in Single Wing is the key to the attack so he will probably emulate the T quarterback in the relative security of the safety position. That leaves the wingback to handle the other defensive halfback spot.

The use of platoons has greatly changed the thinking that, since the war, has determined the choice of offensive linemen. Since it was no longer necessary to consider defensive ability in selecting them, offensive linemen have tended to be smaller than their defensive counterparts. This stems from the fact that speed on offense is so important, and the big fellows are seldom as quick or as fast as their smaller teammates. The formula "impact equals mass times velocity squared" rules over the offense with an iron hand. And the stress on speed has allowed a great many smaller football players to make their varsity teams. A comparatively small guard, quick as a cat, and operating close to the ground, will help the attack much more than a bigger, slower player. Split-second timing demands speed, and the coaches have been turning to the smaller man for this quality on offense.

Offensive guards and tackles in the T must all be good downfield blockers, an accomplishment that demands speed and agility in the open. The blocks on the line of scrimmage do not have to be held long, for the T hits so quickly. Therefore it is the initial impact that is most important—and only the agile player can deliver this. Ends, of course, are still chosen for pass catching ability (and here height is to be considered), but at the same time T ends must be good blockers both on the line and downfield, too. Their overall speed should compare favorably with that of backs, as they must be ball carriers when they catch a pass. Because of the T's balanced formation, ends, tackles and guards will have the same assignments, depending on which side the play is run. In other words, the right guard cannot, ideally, be any slower or less active than the left guard.

In the Single Wing, one guard can be a bit slower than the other—as can one tackle—without great harm being done. It helps, of course, to have all players with speed to burn, but this situation seldom obtains. Their speed may vary, because each man maintains his relative position in the line whether it be in right or left formation. In other words, the long side end is always the long side and whether the formation is long to the right or the left.

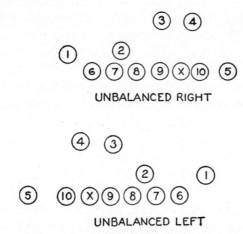

UNBALANCED RIGHT

UNBALANCED LEFT

Diagram 23—Single Wing Formations Unbalanced Right and Left

The diagram shows that the number 6 man and the number 1 man are always together. They block the defensive tackle in when the off-tackle play is run from right formation and they do the same thing when it is run from left formation. Thus, number 5, the short side end, never has to learn how to drive the tackle in with the wingback. He is free to concentrate on other details—and when details are innumerable and practice time is limited, this can be vital. Thus, the "tailback" is always the "tailback," number 10 is always on the "short" side of the center, and numbers 9, 8, 7 and 6 are always to the strength of the formation. This means fewer assignments for the Single Wing linemen. Of course, they must learn to execute the assignments both to the left and to the right, but the actual number of *different* assignments is cut just about in half compared with those most types of T linemen must learn. The use of numbers on the offensive linemen is shown here solely for the sake of clarity.

In Diagram 23, number 5 should be the better pass catcher of the two ends and the better downfield blocker. This is because he is split from the rest of the line and can thus get downfield with less chance of being held up or knocked down on the line of scrimmage. The long side end, number 6, should be the better blocker of the two and is chosen first for his blocking rather than his pass catching ability. Number 5 is likely to be the taller of the two boys, while number 6 will have the sturdier build. Number 7 will be the fastest of the linemen—generally picked from the guard squad—as he will lead the reverses back to the short side and thus has the greatest distance to go. Moreover, the ball carrier he leads will be number 1, the fastest of the backs, and he must not slow the attack. Number 10 will usually be the other guard and he need not be as fast as number 7, for he does not have to run as far to discharge his blocking responsibilities. Number 8 will be the fastest of the tackles—or he may often be chosen from the guard squad if the tackles do not have enough speed. He will lead many of the plays to the long side of the formation and, as he is already on that side, will not have too far to go. Number 9 is the one spot where a comparative slow-poke can play on the offensive line. This man pulls and traps tackles to both sides of the formation. Trapping does not require anything but a straight pull—no necessity for downfield, out in the open, blocking—and the slower player can handle this job. He should have size at this spot because he constantly drives into the defensive tackles—usually the biggest men on the defense—and needs to match their size in order to survive.

The centers in both formations have very special problems. Their first responsibility is to put the ball in play with no mistakes. The T center can be a more effective blocker because he simply hands the ball back to the same man in the same fashion on all types of plays. The Single Wing center must pass the ball back to different men with different pace and depth, depending on the play being run. In order to make his passes absolutely accurate, the Single Wing center must pass with his head down and thus cannot see his blocking assignment in the line. This makes him a less effective blocker than the T center whose head is always up where he can see his opponents' position and judge his charge.

In choosing defensive posts for these linemen, the tackles have generally been the biggest men. They are the backbone of the defensive line, for they are the link between the outside defensive efforts of the ends and the interior work of the guards. Most of the power from both T and Single Wing hits most effectively in their area and they are picked for the size and strength to resist this power. The guards are in a difficult position, too. They are flanked closely on both sides by men who are on the line of scrimmage and thus only a yard from them. They can be "double teamed" by any two of the men in their immediate vicinity. Moreover, straight hitting plays will get to them more quickly than to any other defensive men, since ball carriers need only drive straight ahead to be upon them. The guards are generally a bit smaller than the tackles. They should be more active and built closer to the ground so that they cannot be moved easily by the blockers who get under them. The tackle being a bit further away from the inception point of the attack has more chance to react and make his weight and strength felt.

Speed and agility are the key abilities for defensive ends working in a position which allows a great deal more freedom of movement than at guard or tackle. They must be fast enough to bring down ball carriers in the open field, where runners can dodge much more effectively than when hitting the line. They are picked as good pass rushers—the best pass defense of all! The end gets a better start at rushing the passer than do the linemen who are faced with potential blockers in the open field but he does not have to withstand power blocking of the close order type faced by the other linemen. If defensive linemen are rated on speed and agility, the ends would be in first place, the guards next, and the tackles last. If rated on size and sheer power, it would be tackles first, guards next and ends last. This rule, of course, is general, not infallible.

With the free use of platoons almost completely prohibited by the 1953 rule change, it is necessary for the coaches to consider the above qualifications as ideals—to be hoped for but seldom obtained in a series of compromises. Many fine ball carriers may be forced to ride the bench waiting for spot use while a poorer offensive prospect does the actual playing because his ability on defense gives him an all around edge. The small, active, offensive lineman has seen his best days under two platoons because he does not have the size necessary to hold up on defense. It is now necessary to make sure that in your offensive line you have two men who can handle the defensive tackle positions and two who can play the defensive guard jobs.

And so you can see that the play taking place on the field, the men involved, and the duties they have been given, are the end result of a gigantic task of organization, selection, analysis and teaching that extends over a period of years and into many factors not visible on a stadium field of a Saturday.

Now that you have some of this background in mind, let's proceed to the scene of action for an explanation of its physical setup and regulations.

V Do's and Don'ts

*P*erhaps one of the problems of the human race is that most of us are not very interested in the rules and regulations of anything, but we should be in the rules of a game. Without them there is very little point to the contest. Moreover, if you skip these do's and don'ts you may be passing up the opportunity to be an "authority" in your section of the stands—always an enjoyable experience. In addition, this chapter should help you to take a commanding position in baiting and second-guessing the "umps"—a national pastime for the majority of our sports fans. If you are able to contribute even a minimum of downright knowledge to this highly confused area, imagine your satisfaction and prestige!

1. The Field

The rules governing the playing area, as it is today, are the result of years of change and experimentation. The effort over those years has been to do two things: first, to increase the spectator appeal of the game, and second, to give maximum protection to the players. For instance, it was not until 1933 that the ball was moved ten yards into the field of play after an out-of-bounds had occurred. Prior to that date, the ball had simply been placed just inside the sideline stripe and play had continued in that cramped position. This, of course, limited the effective use of any plays except those aimed at the wide side of the field. The defense invariably overshifted so far to the wide side of the field that the offense was badly handicapped. Moreover, play so near the sidelines was dangerous in that players were constantly being thrown out of bounds in the vicinity of yard markers, stakes and benches. Today the "inbounds lines" are roughly 17 and ⅔ yards in from the sidelines. Any time the ball is downed in the area between these "hash-marks" and the sidelines, the officials place the ball on the same line but 17 and ⅔ yards into the field of play. These "hash-marks" divide the field roughly into thirds which means that the offense is no longer sharply limited in its choice of plays. It is always possible to run either left or right with plenty of room toward the narrow side of the field. This has helped the offense to score by giving it plenty of room in which to operate effectively. On a muddy day, look at the area that gets trampled, and you will see where a game is played.

The gridiron, so-called from its horizontal lines at 5 yard intervals within the 300' x 160' rectangle which is the playing field, was not always thus. Indeed today the 5 yard intervals in the yard lines are a hangover from the days when each team was permitted three downs to make a 5 yard advance—or strangely enough, a 20 yard retreat. Today, the lines might just as well be at ten yard intervals since the offense is now given four tries to make a ten yard advance. No doubt this change would be welcomed by hard-pressed grounds keepers— though they are now comparatively well off. From 1906-1910, in addition to the present lines, there were longitudinal lines, five yards apart, running the full length of the field. This gave the "gridiron" a first rate "checker-board" appearance and must have driven the grounds keepers to distraction.

The purpose was to make sure that the quarterback—who received the ball from the center—would always move a minimum of five yards laterally before starting to gain ground. This rule soon went by the boards as an unwarranted restriction on the offense.

In 1927, the posts, till then situated on the goal line, were moved back ten yards to the "end line." This was done in an effort to protect the players still further. Nothing was more discouraging to a hard working fullback than a head on crash into those posts when blasting into the line for the last precious inches to "pay dirt." Some have felt that this has hurt scoring from the field by place kicks or drop kicks. It is impossible to deny that ten yards has been added to the distance needed for a field goal, but the death knell for field goal scoring was sounded when the forward pass came into its own. The ball is no longer shaped for a kicking game. It is not the same ball that the great kickers of earlier days propelled through the uprights from all angles and from phenomenal distances. Today it is longer, more slender, and a great deal more pointed than the pigskin of old. It is built for passing, not for kicking. The great place kickers at present can be counted on the fingers of one hand. There are no drop kickers plying their trade at all any more; the passers are the ones who get the ball up in the air today. The movement of the goal posts back, then, cannot alone be blamed for the demise of the drop kick. It was a fully justified move to protect the players from possible injury.

In a further effort to protect the players, you will note that all markers along the sidelines have been moved back from the boundaries of the playing area. The flags at the four corners of the field—at the four intersections of the goal lines and the side lines—are mounted on flexible staffs to avoid any chance of injury to a player being forced out of bounds at that spot. The field itself is surrounded on all four sides with a so-called "limit line." This line does not pertain to the game itself, but is designed to keep everyone back from the sidelines except when specifically permitted to be on the field. Although only five feet back from the sidelines this line has produced a safety margin for players and spectators alike in holding back photographers, trainers, managers, spectators and even excitable members of the coaching profession.

2. THE OFFICIALS

There are four of these for any football game and the "men-in-white" are the only non-combatives permitted on the field during actual play. These men have generally been players themselves and have never lost their keen interest in the sport. Theirs is not an easy job—and not one at which anyone is liable to grow rich and fat. For them, officiating is an avocation, and football a stern taskmaster. The rules and interpretations of rules with which they must be familiar fill a booklet of some seventy pages. They must take—and pass satisfactorily—examinations in these rules every year in order to be placed on approved lists of qualified officials. These men must keep in excellent physical condition as they are required to cover ground rapidly in following the play of the game. With the movies recording every movement on the field with pitiless accuracy, these men are graded by all coaches on every game they work. They must be able to take criticism and profit by it. It is really amazing how they cover the field of play. The partisan rooters in the stands would do well to note how perfectly in ninety-nine cases out of a hundred the officials are located to see crucial out-of-bound plays all over the field. This doesn't just happen; it is the result of years of experience and concentration. The problems of controlling players whose emotions are at a fever pitch, of explaining options to them under game pressures demand men of quick, accurate decision and firm, diplomatic manner. There is nothing easy about being an official. People too often remember the inevitable errors and fail to applaud the really surprising amount of technically perfect work done by these men.

What are their duties? In general, all four act as a team to expedite the orderly development of the game. Within the area assigned to them, each man is on the lookout for infractions of the rules. Each carries a "marker"—generally a bit of weighted red cloth—and either a whistle or a horn. The "marker" is dropped to indicate the spot of the foul; while the horn is blown to apprise the referee of the occurrence of a foul. Each official follows the play in his area and is responsible for marking the spot where the ball, or the runner goes out of bounds.

The referee is the captain of the officials. He has the final word on all problems and decisions not specifically assigned to one of the other officials. It is his whistle that you hear signalling the completion of each play. The three other men have horns; and the sound of a horn never stops a play as does the whistle. It merely indicates that there has been an infraction of the rules and a settlement will be arrived at when the play is completed.

The Referee follows the ball like a hawk. His is the responsibility for its position at the conclusion of each play. He starts each play by placing the ball down and then walking away from it. He signals the completion of play by blowing his whistle, and all hostilities should cease at that sound. His position is normally behind the offensive team. Among his many duties is that of exacting penalties and explaining any and all options or alternatives open to either Team Captain. He must inspect the field before play begins and warn of any irregularities. His decisions on balls is final—if wet grounds obtain, he may ask that a dry ball be inserted into the game whenever practical. He must make sure that both teams and his fellow officials are ready before each play.

The Umpire is responsible for the equipment of the players and also for their conduct during the game. His position at the start of each play is behind the defensive line where he concentrates primarily upon the two forward lines to prevent any illegal procedures. He should also help to cover the play after it breaks through the line of scrimmage and develops in his area. His is the most dangerous area in which to operate, since he is in the middle of any run or pass which develops through or over the defensive linemen. Unless extremely agile, this gentleman may find himself knocked down several times in the course of the afternoon and will often return home with assorted bruises as souvenirs.

The Linesman is concerned primarily with violations of the neutral zone—a fancy way of saying offsides—and illegal formations. He has three assistants. Two of these handle the yardage chain and place it at his direction at the proper point to measure progress in any series of downs. The third handles the down indicator. These men must remain off the field unless called for by the Linesman at the Referee's direction. The Linesman must keep himself constantly aware of the progress of the ball in any series of downs and keep accurate count of the downs themselves. He must be sure that the Referee is always clear on the down and yardage to go. His position is in the neutral zone—the same yardline as the ball—but well off towards the sideline out of the way of the players. You will note that if he and his helpers are on your side of the field during the first half, they will be on the opposite side during the second half of the game. This is, no doubt, in the interest of strict impartiality.

The Field Judge has complete authority over the timing of the game and will also cover downfield play in the vicinity of the defensive halfbacks and safety men. He stations himself ten to fifteen yards on the defensive side of the scrimmage line and on the opposite side of the field from the Linesman. He will have a stop watch and will time the game with it, keeping the Referee informed of the time left in each half. If a large scoreboard clock is used—the usual procedure today—

the Field Judge has an assistant on the sidelines who runs it and is responsible to him. The Field Judge, however, must check the clock on all plays and be prepared to take up the timing of the game on his own watch in case it fails to function properly. The Field Judge's position makes him the official arbiter on forward passes and long runs as these plays will occur in his immediate vicinity. In this he takes over for the Referee who is often delayed getting downfield from his position behind the offensive team. In 1953, for the first time, the Field Judge was given a whistle to signal the completion of the long gaining type of plays that occur in his area. In this case he momentarily assumes the responsibilities of the Referee and acts for him on these plays. Diagram 24 shows two teams prepared to start a play from scrimmage showing the proper alignment of the officials for maximum coverage.

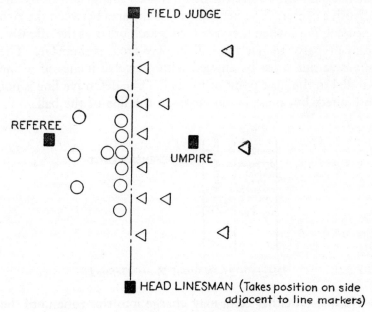

Diagram 24—Officials Position on Field of Play

3. Basic Rules and Penalty Signals

Figure 1—Offside Signal

This signal denotes offside, i.e., a violation of either a scrimmage or a free kick formation. The offside violation of a scrimmage formation means that a player has encroached on the neutral zone before the ball has been snapped back by the offensive center. The neutral zone is the area between the two opposing lines when they are facing each other as the offensive team prepares to put the ball in play from scrimmage. The offensive line must be aligned within twelve inches of a line parallel to the near point of the ball. The defensive line is not so limited, but must be no closer to the line of the ball.

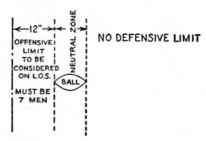

Diagram 25—Neutral Zone Defined

No one on either team may charge into this zone until the ball has been snapped by the center; nor may his head or shoulders encroach upon it even though he does not charge into it. The violation of a free kick formation means advancing beyond the established restraining lines before the ball is kicked. A free kick today occurs only at the start of each half, after each try for point after touchdown, after a successful try for a field goal, and after a safety has been scored. In these cases the neutral zone is the area between the restraining line of the kicking team—which is the yard line on which the ball is placed—and that of the receiving team which is the yardline ten yards from the ball.

Figure 2—Illegal Position or Procedure

This is a rather complicated part of the rules, but the crux of the matter is that at least seven men must be on their scrimmage line for the offensive team. There may be more than seven if you wish, but not less than seven. The scrimmage line for each team "is the yard line and its vertical plane which passes through the point of the ball nearest its own goal-line." An offensive player is considered to be "on his scrimmage line" when he lines up for the play facing his opponent's goal line and with his head or hands not more than twelve inches back from his own scrimmage line. The defense is not limited in any way as to the number they may have on the scrimmage line. They may have none or eleven along that line.

No offensive player along the scrimmage line may receive the ball from the center.

The center, himself, once he has adjusted the ball perpendicular to his scrimmage line may not move it in any manner until he snaps it.

No offensive man may make a false start, or fake a charge, in an effort to draw an opponent offside. Any shift designed to do this, is also illegal.

Figure 3—Illegal Motion or Shift

The rules state that after coming out of the huddle and taking their positions, all offensive players must remain stationary for one full second without movement of the feet, body, head or arms. If a shift is used this one second rule also applies *after the shift*. One man only is permitted to be in motion when the ball is snapped, but his motion must be clearly parallel to, or backward from, the line of scrimmage. If such a player starts from the line of scrimmage, however, he must be five yards behind it when the ball is snapped. That is why most men in motion maneuvers are limited to backs rather than linemen.

Figure 4—Delay of Game

Each team is permitted five free time-outs during the game. When these have been taken, any additional time out for any purpose, other than removal of an injured man from the game, is illegal and will be considered delay of the game.

Each team should have its players on the field and prepared to start the game at the scheduled time at the start of each half.

Twenty-five seconds is allowed the offensive team to start a play after the ball is ready for play. This interval is measured from the time the Referee walks away from the ball after placing it in position for play. If this twenty-five second time limit is exceeded the offensive team is penalized for delay of game.

Any violation of the substitution rule is also deemed delay of the game and penalized accordingly. No substitute shall enter the game while the ball is in play or during the twenty-five second period after the official has walked away from the ball that he has placed ready for play. When a team has exhausted its five free time-outs, substitutions may be made only when the clock is stopped.

Figure 5—Personal Fouls

Personal fouls consist of kicking an opponent, tripping, clipping or piling on after the runner is down. Also, no opponent shall tackle the runner when he is clearly out of bounds or block another man after the whistle has blown ending the play. Any unnecessary roughness shall also be penalized by the officials as a personal foul.

Figure 6—Roughness and Piling On

Although these are personal fouls, they have their own signal in order more clearly to indicate the nature of the foul.

Figure 7—Clipping

This is also a personal foul but has its own signal. Clipping is "throwing the body across or running into the back of an opponent, other than the runner, below the waist." In other words, any block from the rear, where contact is below the waist of the man blocked, is clipping. This rule is put in for the protection of the players and should be carefully observed.

Figure 8—Roughing the Kicker

The kicker, because he is often off balance and in an awkward position at the conclusion of a kick, is protected. Bumping into or knocking down any kicker, or a holder of a place kick, is a foul. If a kick is partially blocked, some slight contact is permissible, but flagrant roughness may even result in the suspension of the rougher from the game.

Figure 9—Unsportsmanlike Conduct

There are a good many items listed in the rule books in this department but essentially the above signal covers any behavior that an official cares to designate as "Unsportsmanlike Conduct." It covers everything from "foul language" to "concealing" the ball beneath the player's clothing. This latter is a real trick with the skin-tight jerseys used today, but was apparently a frequent stratagem in the old days. There must be no coaching from the sidelines at any time. The coaches, players and trainers must not walk up and down or needlessly approach the sidelines. This is to prevent an unscrupulous coach from parading a substitute with #37 on his back up and down the sidelines when he wants his quarterback to run that favorite 37 pass. Another prohibited item is the famous old "hide-out" play where a player, apparently substituted for, suddenly comes to life a yard from the sidelines and races downfield to catch the winning pass. In a nutshell, "Unsportsmanlike Conduct" can cover any attempt to gain an unfair advantage over an opponent. When in doubt an official has the right to hew to the spirit of the rules which certainly never intended such advantages to be taken.

Figure 10—Defensive Holding

Defensive players when attempting to get at a ball carrier may use their hands to "grasp, push, pull or lift offensive players out of the way." If, however, they are not actually making an attempt to get at the runner, they cannot grasp and hold an opponent. This rule is in the book to prevent defensive players from holding or tackling pass receivers who are trying to get downfield for a pass. You can watch for this infraction on pass situation, i.e., late downs with long yardage. Focus on the ends and note the problems they have in fighting clear of the line of scrimmage to get downfield. The defensive men can knock them down by charging or pushing but they should not hold or tackle.

Figure 11—Illegal Use of Hands and Arms

Offensive players, other than the ball carrier, should not use their hands or *extended* arms to block an opponent. In a chest or shoulder block the offensive player must keep his hands in contact with his own body and at no time may the forearm, or elbow, contact the defensive main *above the shoulders*. This is a point that has been much stressed in rules discussions of recent years. The utilization of forearms and elbows in the so-called "stand up" block has been open to wide abuse in that a severe blow can be dealt to an opponent's face or head. A concerted effort should be made to enforce strictly this part of the rule against illegal use of hands and arms—the removal of teeth has no legitimate place on the football field.

Figure 12—Intentional Grounding

A passer who is being rushed hard and trapped far behind his scrimmage line is severely tempted, when unable to find an uncovered receiver, to hurl the ball into any empty part of the field he can see. Unfortunately for the passer, this is illegal. He must steel himself to "eat the ball"—i.e., take his licking, hang onto the ball, and accept the yardage loss as philosophically as his bruises will permit. This rule is an attempt to balance passing offense and pass defense. A good pass rush is still the best defense against a good passer and should not be rendered useless by permitting the passer to ground the ball intentionally.

Figure 13—Illegal Handing Ball Forward or Passing

Two forward passes in the same down are not permitted. If two passes are thrown one must clearly be a lateral, or backward pass, if the other is to be a forward. A forward pass cannot be used on a free kick down. A pass is also illegal when the passer is on his scrimmage line or beyond it when he throws the ball. Handing the ball forward is illegal at any time except when done by offensive players both of whom are at least one yard behind their own scrimmage line.

Figure 14—Forward Pass Interference

There can be no pass interference by either offensive or defensive players. An offensive player cannot "interfere" with a pass defender from the time the ball is *snapped* until it is *touched*. The defensive player cannot "interfere" with a potential pass catcher from the time the ball *leaves the passer's hand* until it is *touched*. This does not mean that offensive linemen cannot interfere with, or block, the defensive linemen pouring in to rush the passer. They can and do, of course. But no blocking or interfering can be practiced on defensive men who are behind their own line of scrimmage— the linebackers, halfbacks and safety man. It is illegal for an offensive end, for instance, to block or hinder the safety man so that the other offensive end may catch the ball in that area without opposition. By the same token the defenders cannot hinder the pass receivers once the ball is in the air. This does not rule out body contact as opponents go up in the air to battle for a high thrown pass. As long as both men are trying for the ball, no foul will be called. Officials generally watch the arms on this play. If both men have their arms stretched high for the ball, body contact is ignored. If one player goes after the ball with only one hand, while the other is on his opponent, that man will generally be called for "interference."

Any player who is in a position to handle any type of kick

before it strikes the ground must be given the opportunity to do so. Any interference with his chance to do this is illegal. He cannot be touched until he has had this opportunity or until the ball has touched the ground. If a punt-catcher signals for a Fair Catch, and races into a crowd to make that catch, it is up to the members of the kicking team to avoid him. If they so much as jostle him they are guilty of interference with his opportunity to make the catch.

Figure 15—Ineligible Receiver Downfield

No ineligible receiver may be beyond the neutral zone until a forward pass has been touched by someone. Ineligible receivers are generally the offensive center, guards, tackles, and any player in a position to accept a hand-to-hand snap from the center. This latter rules out the T formation quarterback as a pass receiver. In these days of numerous flankers, it might be better to think in terms of *who is eligible* to receive passes—all others, then, being ineligible. The only eligible receivers in a pass play are the two men on the *ends of their scrimmage line* whether the regular ends or not and the backs, with the exception noted above.

Figure 16—Ball Illegally Touched, Kicked or Batted

Any eligible player may touch or bat a pass in any direction. Any player may block a scrimmage or return kick. Right here, however, the license to bat or kick the ball around is revoked. Any loose ball during a play cannot be batted or kicked forward along the ground. If the ball pops loose in the end zone, it cannot be batted or kicked either forward or backward. This is designed to keep the game from deteriorating into a violent soccer game whenever the ball is fumbled.

Illegal touching of the ball refers to a player of the kicking team who touches the ball before it touches or it touched by an opponent. You have all seen players of the kicking team huddling over a slowly rolling kick without touching it. The penalty if they do touch it is not great—merely possession of the ball by the opponent at the point of the foul. The opponent gets possession anyway where the ball stops rolling, but the foul of touching it would nullify any other foul which might have occured earlier during the play. For instance, the receiving team may have been offside on the play. If a member of the kicking team touches that ball, his foul nullifies the offside foul. His team will lose the chance to accept the offside penalty which might well give them a First Down and continued possession of the ball. Within the ten yard line, touching the ball illegally makes it a touchback and gives the receiving team possession on its twenty yard line. It is much

better, of course, for the kicking team to leave the ball alone
and hope that it will roll dead somewhere inside that ten
yard line before it rolls into the end zone.

Figure 17—Incomplete Forward Pass, Penalty Declined,
No Play or No Score

In other words, "No Dice!" Best example is given by the
Referee after a try for point after touchdown has failed to
split the uprights.

Figure 18—Crawling, Helping the Runner or Interlocked Interference

Crawling is an attempt by the ball carrier to advance the ball after any part of his body, other than a hand or foot, has touched the ground. This is prohibited in an effort to cut down on piling on a ball carrier.

Offensive players may not push or pull their own ball carrier in an effort to gain more ground. This is also designed to protect the ball carrier by cutting down on the number of men involved in downing him.

The old flying wedge play, where mass interference interlocked itself by grasping straps attached to their teammates' backs, is ruled out today. This type of play was very dangerous as tremendous weight and momentum was built up by such an interlocked mass. Again this prohibition is aimed at protecting the players. No type of interlocked interference is legal today.

Figure 19—Ball Dead

A Dead Ball is a ball not in play. A Live Ball, i.e., a ball in play, is made into a Dead Ball by the Referee's whistle. The Referee "kills" the ball with his whistle.

A Touchback is scored when a team moves the ball over the goal line it is attacking and loses possession of it in the end zone. This can occur on any kick from scrimmage (other than a try-for-point), on a pass, or on a run. Let us give an example of each of these:

1. Team A punts the ball over the goalline that Team B is defending. If the ball is not handled by a Team B player, it is a touchback. If it goes out of play over the end line, it is a touchback. If a team B man catches the ball and is downed in his own end zone before crossing his goalline, it is a touchback.

2. A pass is thrown by Team A into the end zone that Team B is defending. If the pass is intercepted by a Team B man, it is a touchback as long as he downs the ball in the end zone. Indeed he may attempt to run the interception out of the end zone, but as long as he is tackled and downed

before he gets into the field of play, it is still ruled a touch-back.

3. A runner for Team A crosses the goalline defended by Team B. If he retains possession of the ball he, of course, scores a touchdown. If he fumbles, however, and the ball is recovered in the end zone by a Team B player, a touch-back is declared.

After a touchback has been declared, the ball belongs to the team defending that goalline and is put in play by them on their own twenty yard line in whatever manner they see fit. No points are scored on touchback.

Figure 20—Touchdown or Field Goal

A touchdown is scored any time Team A gains or retains possession of the ball in the end zone defended by Team B, counting six big points.

A Field Goal is scored when a drop kick or place kick other than a kick-off or a try-for-point, passes over the bar, or directly over an upright, of the goal attacked by the kicking team. Three points are scored for the kicking team on a successful Field Goal. If the attempt is unsuccessful the kick is treated exactly like any other kick from scrimmage. If it goes into the end zone and is downed or left alone, a touchback is declared. If the ball does not reach the end zone, or goes out of bounds before reaching the end zone, it belongs to the receiving team at that spot. At any time the receiving team may pick up and run with an unsuccessful field goal attempt. If the attempt is successful, the ball is next put in play by a kickoff with the Team Captain of the scored upon team having the choice of kicking or receiving.

Figure 21—Safety

A Safety counts two points and is scored any time that a team is "primarily responsible" for the ball ending up in its possession in the end zone it is defending. This "primary responsibility" falls upon any player who *carries* the ball into his own end zone or who *imparts* to the ball an "impetus" which carries it into his end zone. The impetus given the ball by any player who kicks, passes or fumbles shall be considered responsible for the ball's progress *in any direction* even though its course be deflected or reversed by contact with the ground or another player. Thus, for example, if Team A is kicking from its own end zone, the kick is blocked, and the ball goes out of bounds in that end zone, a safety is scored against Team A. The kicker had "primary responsibility," in this case, for the "impetus" which resulted in the ball going out of bounds in his own end zone. The result would have been the same had the kicker or a teammate succeeded in recovering the blocked kick in the end zone. Had an opponent of the kicker recovered the ball in the end zone, he would have scored a touchdown, of course.

After a safety has been scored, the ball is put in play, by the team scored upon, from its own twenty yard line with a free kick.

Figure 22—Time Out

This signal is given often during a game. The Referee will declare time out whenever a touchdown, Field Goal, Safety or Touchback is scored; when a penalty is incurred; when a pass is ruled incomplete; when a ball or a player goes out-of-bounds during play; when the ball changes hands; and after the kick-off or free kick. These time outs are considered to be Referee's time outs and are not charged to either team. A team uses up one of its five time outs when the Captain asks the Referee for time out, or when a substitute comes into the game while the clock is running but before the ball is ready for play. No substitute shall enter the game when the ball is ready for play and the twenty-five second period started. This would be ruled as illegal delay of the game.

Figure 23—First Down

This signal means that a team possesses a series of "four consecutive scrimmage downs" in which to advance the ball a minimum of ten yards. If they succeed in their effort, they are awarded another First Down and thus retain possession of the ball for another series. If the team fails to gain the stipulated ten yards, their opponents will take over possession of the ball with a First Down of their own.

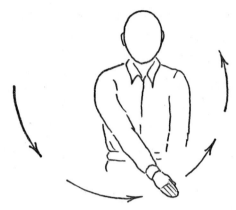

Figure 24–Start the Clock or No More Time-outs Allowed

This signal is given by the Referee to start the clock whenever it has been stopped:

1. By a time out or an illegal delay.
2. To award a first down.
3. At the Referee's discretion.

On all other occasions, such as a score, an out-of-bounds, an incomplete pass or a penalty, the clock starts automatically with the snap of the ball. When a team has exhausted its five free time-outs, no more will be allowed except for the benefit of an injured player.

You are now versed in the terminology, organization and rules of the game. You are prepared to follow the why of a game, but do you know how to watch one in progress? From here we must go into a discussion of what to look for on the field of play.

VI Don't Watch the Ball

$\mathcal{D}$on't watch the ball! This may seem strange advice for following a game in which the main object is the movement of a ball over a given area. After all, you say, what else should you be watching? This is what you came to see.

Granted that the movement of the ball is of prime importance, narrow concentration on it eliminates much vital action and many of the group and individual efforts taking place at the same time. Because of the elements of deception in modern football, many spectators feel that their only hope in following the game is to watch the ball. How else, they say, can they understand the strategic moves, study the T quarterbacks, passers and ball carriers and evaluate the stars in the game in "all-time" ratings? What is the value of the alternative to concentrating on the ball?

Paradoxically, *not* watching the ball can help you to follow its movement and to understand more fully how and why that movement takes place. Football is a team game, with the efforts of eleven men on each side all carefully planned in relation to the movement of the ball. Their actions can give an advance tip on the course the ball will follow and ability to

take in the team effort can immeasurably enrich your understanding and enjoyment of the game. In the following pages,
we will outline methods by which keen students of the game
look for these extra elements that are all important to it. Try
them yourself and see how much more enjoyment you get
out of your Saturday afternoons.

1. Deception in the Stands as Well as on the Field

Are you helping to fool yourself when you take your seat in
the stands? Many spectators fail to follow a game properly
through neglect of some fairly simple background factors that
can add much to the enjoyment. The crowd in the stands is a
very real part of the spectacle that is modern football, and its
thorough, alert participation in the drama being unfolded on
the field is an important element in the game's hold on the
imagination of the public.

Even a football coach has to admit that many in the crowd
are there for reasons other than the technical appreciation of
a complicated game. Pretty girls wearing flowers perhaps
spend most of their time looking at the clothes of other pretty
girls wearing flowers, and their main delight in a well executed
forward pass is the chance it gives to jump up and down and
give their dates a hug.

For those who come as serious fans, there are many distractions, starting with the weather, arranging for baby sitters,
fighting game day auto traffic, and carrying right through to
poor seats, souvenir and hot dog vendors waving their wares
under your nose, back-slapping old grads and the arrival of
latecomers well into the second quarter (those same people
who start leaving late in the third quarter). We are not able
to help you out of all these complications, but, recognizing
them, we can suggest a few ways to prepare yourself, as a
spectator, to help keep you from being fooled.

Earlier chapters have covered the routine that goes on the
year round in preparation for putting the team before you in a

stadium. An appreciation of all this is a great help in following the game. That oft-heard remark about what a soft racket
coaches must have for the nine months when football is not
in season is a good indication of how a spectator can fool
himself. As we have already shown, off-season organization
can very possibly mean the difference between defeat and
victory. A sympathetic understanding of this program can
answer many of Saturday's questions.

It is also a big handicap to come to a game in ignorance of
the rules and the role of the officials. Few spectators will go
so far as to memorize all the hand signals for penalties, but a
general familiarity with them is a help. They have already
been covered in Chapter V, and your game program will have
a page on which they are pictured for quick reference. Officials come in for a lot of abuse which is very seldom de-
served. An understanding of the scope of their duties and
the generally efficient way in which they do a tough job can
keep you abreast of things when they tend to become confusing.

Familiarity with the type of formations you are going to see
in a given game gives you a good head start on the elements of
the contest and we have already tried to outline the basic
thought behind the main systems.

If you can plan your Saturday to get ahead of last minute
traffic jams and take your seat early, you will get in an another
very important tip-off to serious football students—the pre-
game warm-up session. No good football scout ever misses
this chance to get more data on the individuals on a team.
Checking them against their program listing and watching
them as they punt, pass, catch or go through line drills gives
an idea of what to look for from them in game action. The
groups that operate together in warm-up drills usually indicate
what substitutions to expect. And an especially keen observer
may be able to tell the ultimate outcome of a game through

the difference in the spirit and organization shown by the teams before the game.

These are some of the factors that can prepare a spectator for fuller enjoyment of his Saturday afternoons before the kick-off. The next step is the actual viewing of the game and some advice on how you can train your faculties to help you.

2. How to Watch the Game

Football scouts are often asked: "What do you look for in a game and how do you see so much?" Scouts have special problems and do not watch a game as ordinary spectators, but it is true that they can see much more than the average fan. Each one has different pet tricks and theories, and thought differs in various schools of football across the country on the major items to look for, but there is one basic principle that applies to all viewing of football games—the proper use of vision.

This may sound like a highly complicated and unnecessarily technical worry for the average fan, but it does not have to be. In World War II, the services developed techniques for recognition of ships and aircraft through visual aids that proved how most people fail to make full use of their visual faculties. With no previous training, most men were able to grasp the technique of flash recognition of aircraft and ship silhouettes and the visual remembrance of ten digit numbers flashed on a screen for a brief interval.

Transference of this ability to the watching of football, or any other game, can be an important aid in getting more out of what goes on before your eyes. To get a bit technical about it, there are two elements to consider: the scope of your peripheral vision and the ability to concentrate on one axis.

The human eye is merely a camera, optically. Vision is the formation of images in the mind, transferred from reception in the eye of light rays reflected from the surface of objects. As a camera, the eye is photographically limited to a certain periphery, or outer limit of scope. It is possible to train the eye to broaden this scope and get the overall effect of a large scene. You can test the extent of your own peripheral vision very simply. Stand erect with your arms extended straight out in front and look at your hands. Keeping your eyes on this line of sight, spread your arms to the side. The point at which you can no longer see your hands is the limit of your peripheral vision. The same thing applies to moving one arm up and one down. It is probably a much wider scope than you had realized and indicates the extent of the full capabilities of your eyes.

Using this visual ability involves the choice of an axis of concentration, along with an attempt to see the picture as a whole image. It takes conscious effort to get used to this procedure, but the habit can become second nature with practice.

3. Using the Eyes to Watch a Game

Of course, the axis of concentration is different from each seat and on each play. Like harried athletic directors trying to allot tickets to angry alumni, we could wish here that every seat was on the fifty yard line; and for purposes of explanation, let's take the ideal situation of a play on the fifty yard line as seen from a fifty yard line seat. Diagram 26, page 114, shows the application of this axis concentration theory. In Part A, the light area between the forty-nine yard line is the containing focal point. Whatever the eyes see along this line is the first important picture for them to record. From a grandstand seat all the players along this line can be brought into the picture. The upward-downward range of vision should be centered on a line running horizontally through the ball.

Peripheral vision on the left should take in the deepest man in the offensive backfield. To the right, it should encompass

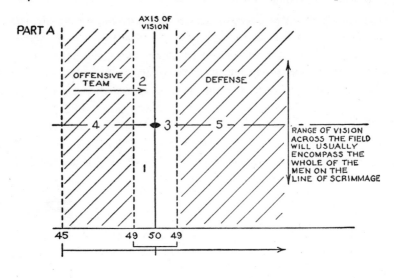

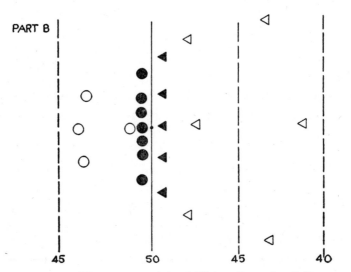

Diagram 26—Axis of Vision, Part A and B

as many of the defensive players as the individual's scope permits. In Part B, a typical alignment of players in such a situation, the blacked-in circles and triangles represent the men on whom your eyes should concentrate, letting peripheral vision take care of as many of the white circles and triangles as possible.

Within this field of vision there are varied elements of play taking place, and to follow a play a good opening trial might be to concentrate on sectors one through five in that order, as shown on the diagram. Observation of a small area can help a spectator to pick out the component parts of the action.

Within the axis, the play of the game, divided into the two simple categories of running and passing plays, can be recognized quickly. Kicking plays, of course, are usually tipped off by special formations.

Picking out running plays involves an observation of the general flow of the play. Blocking effort is the key to running plays. There is almost always a blocking effort at the point of opening, with the main concentration to the inside, or toward the center of the focal area. In addition to point-of-opening blocking effort, there must be an accompanying effort against the defensive secondary to spring the runner beyond the primary opening. These blocking efforts should focus attention on the ultimate direction of the play.

At the primary opening there will be a block in and a block out. Most of the blocks out are made by pulling linemen, so their movement will indicate the direction. Quick analysis of their lateral movement will help shift your eyes quickly to the blocking concentration. In most plays there will be a release of men into the defensive secondary through the line of scrimmage, for which the technical term is "flow of play." It is a telltale giveaway, because the attacking sector will almost certainly not be on that side. In summary, then, look for these three factors to determine the direction of a running play:

a. Concentration of blocking effort.
b. Lateral movement of pulling linemen.
c. Release of men downfield on side away from play.

Passes can be tipped off for the spectator by the same line of deduction. Most teams protect passers with a retreating type of block. With it there will be no telltale concentration of blocking effort. Linemen will pull, but a quick glance in the direction of their motion does not bring us to a center of effort. There is also no flow of play downfield by linemen other than ends. Here, then, are the determining factors for picking out a passing play:

a. Absence of blocking concentration.
b. Distinct change in type of blocking effort.
c. Absence of flow of play.

This general recognition helps in picking out the other elements of play more quickly. In a running play, primary observation showing that the play is directed at sector 1, as shown in diagram, enables us to shift our eyes to the backfield maneuver in progress and to realize that the back heading for that sector will most probably be the ball carrier. In a pass situation, the best procedure is to follow the course of receivers on their way downfield and then shift back to the offensive backfield. This is the quickest method of evaluating whether the receivers are covered properly or not.

By systemizing observation of play in this manner, the whole picture can be comprehended and most of the detailed incidents of blocking, ball carrying, passing and receiving easily filled in. As an example, long after a play has ended, you may note that the offensive left guard in Part B of Diagram 26 is getting up off the ground with the defensive left end, which indicates that blocking the end was his assignment.

If, through your concentration on the axis of the play, your first recollection was of the guard pulling right, followed by a six yard gain inside the left defensive end, and no one went outside that end, you can conclude that the left guard has done a fine job of blocking. You may even have seen him at it. On the other hand, if there had been a back circling outside the defensive end, then faking must have set up the end for a successful block. In either case, team conception of the play was good.

Tying together all these threads gives the spectator an increased opportunity to analyze the play and judge the excellence of its execution. In this manner it can be decided whether individual brilliance or team effort was responsible for offensive success, and whether defensive strength, or weakness of offensive conception has made certain plays fail.

Continuing this line of thought, we can now go into the specific elements of the different offensive systems.

4. What to Watch for in Single Wing

The general heading of "Single Wing" still covers a variety of coaches' systems, no two of which are exactly alike. The public likes to think of Single Wing football as containing power, the standard off tackle play, and emphasis on the running pass. Some Single Wing teams may lack one or more of these, but they still fall in the category.

Power is the keynote, with deception second. The formation is noted for power blocking. The use of deception aids in setting up the application of power and promotes the delay needed to have the power take effect.

A. Line Openings

These have a direct relation to the backfield maneuver being used. Focusing on an axis of sight along the scrimmage line, as previously outlined, brings us to the area where the play unfolds; at the opening in the line.

Straight Hitter. In this type of play there are no pulling linemen and very little deception is involved. The backfield

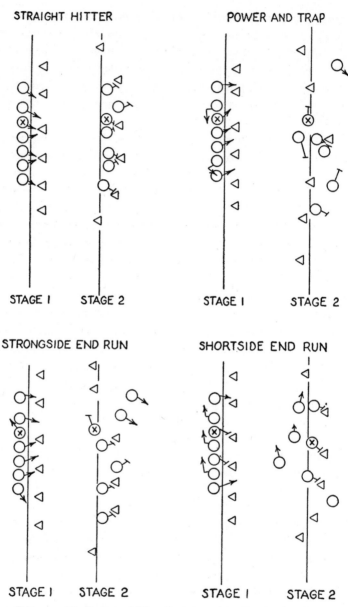

Diagram 27—Stages of Play Development, Line Movements

maneuver hits directly into the line, where the attempt is to move the play forward by the sheer force of knocking the defense back. There is a blocking concentration at the point of opening, and the fringe efforts are directed at steering the defense away from this point. With no real flow of play, one or two men may be released into the secondary defense on each side of the opening. Diagram 27, page 118, shows a typical straight hitter as viewed on the axis in two stages; initial movement and the establishment of contact.

Power and Trap. In this general type of opening, the block to the inside at the opening is a two-on-one power block designed to move the defender backward and laterally. The block out is a position block effected by a pulling lineman or a back moving laterally—sometimes two men in these categories. It is successful if the blocker gets inside position. Diagram 27, also shows the two stages of a typical play using this kind of opening.

End Run. Since there are no men in position to get an initial block at the opening, this is a different type of play. Backs or linemen move wide and deep, laterally, to get position on the end. The direction of this movement, the flow of the play, and the absence of blocking concentration indicate the end to be run. Diagram 27, page 118.

B. Backfield Maneuvers (Diagram 28)

Fullback Bucks. These are straight ahead line plunges behind straight hitter openings. The ball comes directly to the fullback from center and he runs right to the blocking effort.

Straight Tailback Series. The tailback takes a direct pass from center and runs inside or outside of tackle or around the end. He can also handoff to the wingback for a reverse to the short side of the formation. There can be a straight hitter series for the tailback but it is not used often.

Fullback Spin Series. This is the most frequently used spin series in the Single Wing. There is also a tailback spin series with full and half spins but it is not seen much. In the fullback full spin, he fakes first to the tailback and keeps the ball, carrying between the guards or inside tackle. He can also give the ball to the tailback for an off tackle or end run play, or to the wingback for a reverse. He can also work these fakes and handoffs from a half spin.

The Buck Lateral. This combines the features of straight hitters and spin reverses with the threat of a T quarterback. The fake or actual ball exchange between the fullback and blocking back is made close to the line of scrimmage as in the T.

C. Passing

The Single Wing is especially advantageous for passing because three receivers, the ends and wingback, are in a position to get downfield quickly. Passes can be thrown from any of the above backfield maneuvers with the added threat of a fourth receiver getting downfield.

Running Passes. These develop from the straight tailback series with either the tailback or wingback throwing. Tip-off that it will be a pass rather than a run is the absence of flow of play.

Spin and Buck Lateral Passes. These are under the same general category in which the execution of the pass is delayed for a short time. The ultimate objective of the pass is disguised until the spin or buck fake is completed, immobilizing the defense while the offense gains an advantage.

Straight Drop Back Passing. Either the tailback or fullback takes a direct pass from center and fades to throw. He has a full view of the receivers and the deployment of the defense while preparing to pass.

5. What to Watch for in the T (Diagram 29)

It might almost be better to stay "what to watch for in the T quarterback." Deception is the byword in the T formation, and this man is the initiator and the key to all the deception.

STRAIGHT HITTERS

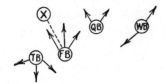

TAILBACK STRAIGHT SERIES

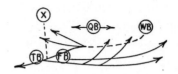

FULL SPIN SERIES

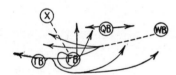

HALF SPIN SERIES

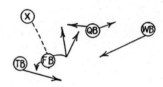

BUCK LATERAL SERIES

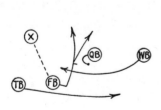

STRAIGHT PASSING

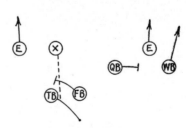

Diagram 28—Single Wing Backfield Maneuvers

As opposed to Single Wing, power and deception are in exactly the reverse ratio. T coaches often say they prefer this system because the players enjoy fooling the opposition, and also because deception both fascinates young players and keeps older players continually on their toes.

A. Elements of Deception

The T quarterback operates on the edge of that axis of vision we have been discussing. The different types in this category fall under two general headings.

Sliding or Straight T Quarterback. This type moves with the ball in a direct lateral movement from the center. He does not turn his back to the line of scrimmage even when dropping back to pass, similar to straight passing in the Single Wing.

Pivoting T Quarterback. He uses a reverse pivot putting his back to the line of scrimmage and making his fakes in this position. He drops to pass after completing these fakes, somewhat akin to spin and buck lateral passes in Single Wing.

B. Backfield Maneuvers

All T quarterbacks fake certain basic backfield maneuvers. For purposes of classification, they can be generalized as follows.

Handoffs. An exchange of the ball from the quarterback to another back moving straight ahead. The quarterback hands the ball immediately after moving from his original position under center without prior fakes. If he does fake first and then makes a handoff, it is called a delayed handoff.

Pitchout. A quick toss out to either a halfback or fullback running directly to circle an end. Prior faking creates a delayed pitchout.

Crossbuck. Here the ball carrier slants behind another back and runs to the opposite side. The fake can be made to one or two men while the ball carrier delays and then receives the ball while running across the direction of the fake. This is a delayed hitter.

Three-Way Maneuver. Here there are three distinct fakes. The primary fake is followed by a second one, which might involve exchange of the ball. The third fake or "give" is in the direction of the original fake. Power and trap plays in T formation develop from this. If the play goes through the trap it is a fake pitchout. If the pitchout is made it is a delayed trap pitchout.

Quarterback Option. This can develop from any maneuver. The quarterback can make one or two fakes and then decide to keep the ball. The Split T makes wide use of this play.

Combinations. Plays can develop out of a combination of these maneuvers. An end run or off-tackle play can derive from a handoff or crossbuck. For example, a handoff or crossbuck can be faked, followed by a handoff to the ball carrier on the same side.

C. Line Openings

Line openings in the T are governed by the speed desired in running off plays. It is helpful in looking for eventual openings to know the maneuvers used in making them.

One Versus One. Most of the openings in which the ball carrier comes into the line quickly are based on this type of blocking. It is hard to pick out any concentration of blocking, but the quarterback and ball carrier also converge on this spot quickly. Handoffs with any type of quarterback, and most plays with a sliding quarterback, are based on this kind of opening.

Power and Trap. The T also uses this Single Wing specialty. More often than not the power block will not be a double block, however, but a single block-in at the opening. The primary movement and fake of the quarterback supplements the blocking effort. Pulling linemen are used to effect the block-out at the opening.

SLIDING T QB

PIVOTING T QB

HANDOFF

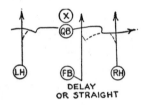

DELAY
OR STRAIGHT

PITCHOUT

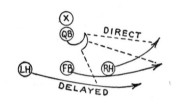

CROSS-BUCK OR X-BUCK

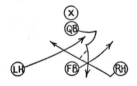

CROSSBUCK OR X BUCK

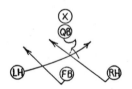

3 WAY MANEUVER

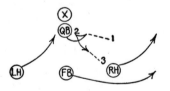

HANDOFF OFF TACKLE

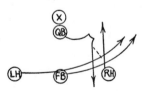

Diagram 29—T Formation Backfield Maneuvers

Cross Blocking. This is a variation of one versus one. At the point of opening, two men block obliquely, with one stepping behind the other to hit the defensive man from a side angle. The quarterback and ball carrier arrive quickly, but not with the speed of the handoff play.

End Runs and Sweeps. These have the same characteristics as in the Single Wing. The flow of the play and the depth of the backfield for making blocks are both visible and there is very little blocking effort in the line.

D. Passing

In the balanced T, the passing threat is basically the same as spin passing from the Single Wing. However, since the ends are the only receivers able to move downfield at the snap of the ball, most passes from this formation develop out of initial threats created by quarterback fakes and backfield maneuvering. Flankers and men-in-motion can be used to get three or more receivers downfield.

With a sliding T quarterback, running passes and direct drop-back passes are most effective. A pivoting quarterback primarily makes use of delay and deception in developing his passing plays.

6. How to Analyze an Unorthodox Formation

So far we have tried to cover the generalities of the main basic systems in modern football. It would be impossible to go into all the variations on them, such as the Single Wings of Tennessee, Michigan, Michigan State, Southern California, Princeton, Penn and Harvard, or the T's of Stanford, Notre Dame, Oklahoma, California, Illinois, Wisconsin, Yale and Cornell. There are other offshoots, such as the Winged T of Penn State, Boston University and Columbia, or the Texas Christian and Southern Methodist spreads. The mere listing of all these (and there are many more) should indicate that there is really no "orthodox" football formation, but rather that each one is an expression of individual coaching genius. Our outline has been aimed at watching any formation based on generally similar systems, but occasionally something that does not fit neatly into any of these categories comes on the scene. For example, the I Formation sprung by Notre Dame in recent years. The methods we have given for watching a game can still be applied to analysis of something like this, and you need not be left in the dark. Our own experience with the I Formation is limited to viewing of newsreel and television pictures and through discussion with other coaches, but the basic principles of what to look for in watching a game can still be applied.

The first place to look is along that axis of concentration, where we find a balanced line with splits. The backfield lines up back of center in a column, so that the quarterback is still, in effect, a T quarterback. We should, therefore, look primarily for deception, rather than power.

The general order of the backs behind the quarterback is halfback, fullback, halfback. How close the first halfback stands behind the quarterback will indicate whether the quarterback will slide or pivot. If the men are too close to him to give him time to pivot for handoffs, he will probably be a slider. With no direct handoffs possible, he will use slant handoffs, hitting fast behind one versus one or cross blocking. The primary running threat would be between the tackles, with end runs developing out of fake cross bucks, using delayed pitchouts.

Analysis of what to expect from passing in this formation can also follow lines of deduction already explained. Since only two receivers are in position to go downfield immediately, all of the passing from I Formation should require a delay. With backfield men relatively closer to the scrimmage line than in the T, it approaches the Single Wing in ability to get a third man downfield. Passing would follow the procedures of a balanced T fairly closely, with the quarterback faking a run maneuver and then wheeling out to one side to throw. You could probably expect the halfback behind him to head in the opposite direction from his handling, and either the fullback or the deep halfback to go out in the flat on the same side as the quarterback.

Since delay is necessary in setting up I Formation (Diagram 30) passes, while the running game gives the quarterback the opportunity to send his best ball carrier to either side, with good deception, our theories of what to look for in a game should lead you to expect more running than passing when you see this formation in use.

And so you can equip yourself for an intelligent understanding of even the most complicated and unusual maneuvers on offense. Offense is only half the battle, though, and a full appreciation of the contest calls for a similar approach to the problems of defense.

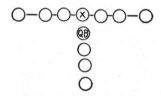

Diagram 30—Special Formation—"I" Formation

VII Keep Up Your Guard— The Defense

So far, we have been primarily concerned with offense. It is the positive side of the game; and since it is the main instrument of scoring, it is the phase of football that comes in for the most attention and discussion. When you go to a game, it is the offense with which you want to keep up, and which presents you, as a spectator, with the more interesting problems of understanding and interpretation.

However, since there must be two sides to every contest, there cannot be a full appreciation of the sport unless both sides are understood. The history of football, as we have pointed out, has been one long struggle for domination between offense and defense. If either one seemed on the verge of becoming overly favored, adjustment was made. Defensive skills, and the swing of the pendulum in favor of defense, have been the major determining factors in developing the offensive formations and systems we have outlined in previous chapters.

Although it was caused by other considerations, the return to one platoon football in 1953 would seem to have been an adjustment in favor of the defense, and this side of the game has thereby assumed added importance. There are several reasons for this. First, defensive skills come more naturally, and a coaching staff, limited in its time, will pick the players who have natural ability in this field, so that greater time can be spent in coaching them on offensive assignments. Also, most players inherently prefer defense and feel more at home at it, and it is bound to be favored in a one platoon system.

In addition, the two-platoon era, with the opportunity it brought for concentrated coaching in single phases of the game, created a new specialist, the defensive coach, whose duty it was to spend all his time thinking up ways to stop the offense. The natural result was a development of defense to a refinement never before possible. These theories are now a permanent part of the overall science of the game and can still be applied to coaching the defense, despite the reduction in time available for the purpose.

For the spectator watching a game, defense may seem easier to follow because all the average fan wants to know is "who made the tackle?," or "who broke up the pass?" Tackling and pass interception are the most spectacular facets of defense, just as ball-carrying and passing are on offense. However, just as we have advised you "don't watch the ball," in showing you how to achieve maximum understanding of the offense, so can we point out that there are many contributing factors to a good tackle or pass interception that the spectator should know how to analyze. Why does a certain player get his name announced repeatedly over the public address system as the tackler? Is he an outstanding star, or is he merely fulfilling an assignment in which several other players have an unpublicized but important part? Why does a team vary its line up on a defense in certain situations and in certain parts of the field? There is a lot more here than meets the eye of the observer who just watches a ball carrier being tackled or a pass being knocked down.

If you will check back to the section of Chapter VI dealing with the use of vision, the theories outlined there should be applied to defense as well. While you are "not watching the ball," your peripheral vision should be taking in some actions of the defense as shown in Diagram 26, page 114.

This use of peripheral vision, in watching defense, brings up an advantage that the stadium spectator has over the home television viewer. Television cameras lack "peripheral vision" as they are normally used to cover football. Most of the time they cut off a view of the defensive secondary, the men behind the scrimmage line, preventing the observer from knowing the type of defensive alignment and from following the actions of the secondary while a play is developing.

In watching a defense, you will not see as many distinctive evidences of a coach's personal genius as in offensive formations. Because there is less need for variety and surprise, and because defensive skills are basically somewhat simpler and require less coaching, defensive play is generally more standardized than the offense. This is only a matter of degree, however, as variety and surprise do enter into defense.

We have referred to offense as the "positive side of football." This would make defense a negative function, which is true in that its primary purpose is to prevent scoring by the other team. However, since the other team cannot make a touchdown when you have possession of the ball, your own defense does have a positive function in complementing the offense. Its effectiveness in quickly regaining control of the ball by forcing the opposition to give it up determines the number of opportunities its own offense has and it can also directly account for scores by intercepting passes, blocking punts and recovering fumbles and forcing safeties.

These are called "breaks," but no defensive planning is complete without some specific thinking on how these breaks can be forced.

1. Defensive Fundamentals

In newspaper accounts of early season practice sessions you often see that a coach "stressed fundamentals" during a workout. Sometimes, particularly if a team has met with a Saturday disaster, this phrase will be repeated on into November, usually concerning a Monday or Tuesday session.

The frequency with which these words might lead cynical fans to assume that they are a catch phrase akin to a politician "pointing with pride" or "mending his fences," but there is no getting away from the fact that a team must be well-grounded in "fundamentals" to achieve success. Every good coach does "stress" them. He can burn the midnight oil thinking up the most brilliant strategy in the world, but it all goes for naught if his charges do not block and tackle.

The individual defensive aptitudes are basic. Good tacklers and pass defenders are born, but they can be improved; and men who were not so gifted naturally can be trained to better things.

Tackling. If a player does not like tackling, if he fails to get a thrill from a hard, clean tackle, he is probably wasting his time in the game. The contact involved and the feeling of physical accomplishment it brings are one of the basic appeals of the game. For the spectator, too, good tackling can be a source of satisfaction, while watching sloppy tackling is a distressing experience.

Tackling is good if it is decisive. Generally, to stop a ball carrier, tackling must aim at cutting off his locomotive power —"neutralizing" his legs. This is not always possible. A big tackle cannot often get low enough to handle a small scat back in this way, but where the players are of similar size it is the main objective.

The shoulder tackle is the best of all. The defender meets the ball carrier as they move straight at each other. The tackle is made by driving the shoulder into the ball carrier's upper thighs and reaching out to encircle and grasp his legs at the same time. The arms have an uprooting force on the runner's legs, and the shoulder drive topples him over. When properly executed, this is a beautiful tackle and ends things right there; no more ground gained beyond point of contact. Unfortunately for the defense an opportunity for such clear-cut execution does not often occur. When it does, the thud can be heard in the upper stands and a gasp escapes from the crowd.

All other forms of tackling are derivatives. They depend on the relative position, speed and direction of runner and tacklers, and timing enters into the problem. The ability of a ball carrier to ruin a tackler's timing is a frequent cause of the missed tackles you see. The side tackle is the basic one in this situation. Here the runner is moving obliquely away from the tackler, who then tries to get his body across and in front of the runner's legs to hobble them as the arms encircle them, tripping the far leg and bending the near one laterally so that the tackle evolves into a falling, rolling movement of runner and tackler.

If it has been done properly, the tackler ends up with both arms wrapped around the lower portion of the runner's legs while he is on top of them. Most tackles end up as something between a shoulder tackle and a side tackle, but every football fan can probably remember when a long arm, clutching desperately at anything it could grasp from neck to toe, saved a tough situation. Expediency creates its own theory, or as someone once said, "necessity is the mother, etc."

Getting in Position to Tackle. This involves preliminary timing, or working out a "collision course" with the runner, but it also means mental diagnosis of the play and physical shedding of blockers while en route to the point of contact. An instinctive tendency to protect one's legs through footwork and use of hands, and a sense of timing, are the greatest aids here, along with use of that peripheral vision we have been telling you to put in play from your seat in the stands.

Ability to see someone slanting in from the side for a block helps a defensive player in protecting himself. These skills can be developed through coaching and practice, and a coach can also cut down or increase an individual's responsibilities according to his talents.

Grandstand critics have been known to hop on a publicized defensive star for seeming lapses in his play, not realizing that, because of his ability, the coach has given him extra responsibility in the usual areas of weaker players.

Ability to Defend Against Passes. This is a facet of the game that causes coaches more woe than almost any other. Every fan seems to think that his own team has the nation's worst pass defense. It is a curious psychology, stemming from the fact that a completed pass is usually the most dramatically damaging kind of play, often changing what seemed like a safe situation in the flash of an eye. The interested rooter is disposed to feel that passing success by his own team is due to fine execution, while that of an opponent is purely traceable to the lapses of his team's defense.

Actually, pass defense, as an individual skill, can only be coached to a certain point. Beyond that it is an instinctive trait that some otherwise finely endowed players lack. It can take two fundamental forms; denying the ball to the receiver by knocking it down, or by interception. Breaking up a pass is purely a contest between two individuals, while interception involves a sense of timing and catching ability.

Not so fundamental are speed and a play-diagnosis sense, but these may be used to overcome the basic lack of fundamental skills. A man with good speed can make up for lack of diagnostic sense, and one who is not inherently able to put up a good contest for the ball can partially overcome this by being in the right spot at the right time.

2. POSITION PLAY

From these general fundamentals of defensive play, the next step is a study of the positions in which they are used, followed by an outline of what to look for in team alignments of these different positions. Modern developments have done a pretty good job of mixing up the old standard designations of defensive positions, but they still bear more relation to their familiar names than they do on offense. We have seen in an earlier chapter the general physical types that coaches try to fit into the various categories. Remembering that, in modern football's giant mixer, ends now sometimes drop back as halfbacks, making ends out of tackles, while guards and tackles drop in and out of the line, sometimes becoming linebackers depending on the alignment, these then are the fundamentals of play at the various positions:

End Play. The basic premise of end play is not to be taken in, literally and figuratively. If an end does find himself being outmaneuvered and forced to the inside, he must try to effect a forceful delay by taking interferers out of the play. He must always protect his legs from blockers who have an outside angle. Methods differ on depth of penetration and footwork, but an end will usually have room to maneuver and use his hands to ward off blockers and contain the play to the inside. Ends may have other assignments, depending on the area a play strikes, and on pass defense you will see them used for everything from rushing the passer to dropping back as a secondary defender, but this ability to keep his flank from being turned while using up the effectiveness of blockers is paramount.

Tackle Play. Since the end's main responsibility is to turn plays to the inside, the offense naturally will follow by trying to apply power at that spot. The off-tackle power play is one of the oldest in football and its use has determined the type of player in the tackle position: big, rugged and strong. Teams without the power to handle tackles with direct blocking often use guile, allowing the big boy to penetrate and then cutting him down with a side block after he had fallen into the trap. Modern tackle play, therefore, requires the ability to withstand power blocks and to employ a controlled charge to avoid being trapped.

Guard Play. This is typified by hard, low, aggressive play in expectation of power plays launched at these positions. The ability to "dig in" is all important here. Fewer direct tackles will be made by men in this position, but agility can be used to advantage in following plays that hit other sectors.

Secondary. Although including all defenders who are not on the line of scrimmage, this is not a specific term because the composition varies depending on the alignment. The function of the secondary is to close any gaps in the primary defense exploited by the offense. It requires good tacklers. Pass defense ability is basic. There are three divisions of the secondary: linebacker, halfbacks and the safety man.

Linebackers. Look for the best tacklers and soundest players on a squad in this spot. It is a rugged position, demanding size, speed, diagnostic sense and an ability to ward off blockers. A linebacker has to like to mix it, but he can't be a slam-into-'em boy disregarding all other considerations. Pass defense is a very important function of a linebacker in today's game, and many of the famous roving centers of years gone by would not be up to the present requirements of the job.

Halfbacks. Defense is a question of planned areas of support, and the halfbacks support the ends on running plays. You will see some of the best open field tackling by defensive halfbacks. If the end has absorbed and delayed the effectiveness of the blockers leading a ball carrier, it is the halfback behind him who moves up fast to make the tackle, often a spectacular one. Don't forget the job that the end did in setting up the situation, however. Speed and a good sense of play-diagnosis are other traits to look for in defensive half-backs.

Safety Man. In the planned support structure, he supports everyone generally and the halfbacks specifically. The type of play required from him is similar to that of the halfbacks, but he will not be in as much contact (you hope). A recent trend has been to move the safety man nearer the line of scrimmage, often up even with the halfbacks. He is generally more effective here on tackling and pass defense, and "team defense," the dropping back of players who find that their own sectors are not threatened by the direction of a play, helps to cover the deeper area. The close safety man is vulnerable to a quick kick, but the emphasis on possession in modern football has cut down on the use of this stratagem.

3. DEFENSIVE ALIGNMENTS

We now come to the methods used in spacing and positioning the players and making use as a team of the fundamentals outlined above. There are certain patterns which, through common usage, have become "orthodox." They will be fairly familiar to most football fans, and all serve as a basis for many of the combinations and variations that have come into use lately. Most offensive systems are predicated on these orthodox defenses and will equip themselves with plays designed to work against the different patterns.

Defensive alignments are designated by a combination of numbers that is practically self-explanatory. In looking at a formation, just count the number in each group from the line of scrimmage out, to determine what the alignment is. The first number is that of men on the line of scrimmage, followed by the number of linebackers, halfbacks and safety men in that order (or at least the combination of the secondary if these positions are mixed in together). Here are the most frequently seen standard ones:

Six-Two-Two-One. This means six men on the line, two

linebackers, two halfbacks and a safety man. It is the most commonly used defense, one you will see more often than any other. Why should it be?

The defense must plan for running and passing threats, and the 6-2-2-1 presents the most effective defensive balance toward a balanced attack. It has six men on the line to handle running threats, with linebackers to plug any gaps, halfbacks back of each end to support them, and a man deep to take care of long threats. Since three is usually the number of pass receivers sent deep into a secondary, there are an equal number of deep men to take care of the situation, utilizing the two halfbacks and safety man.

Five-Three-Two-One. Taking a man from the line to use as a linebacker is fairly common. You will see this alignment when there is a good possibility of passes but with the threat of a run still to be guarded against. The 2-1 deep secondary is still standard, but the added linebacker helps to cover the shallow areas better against short passes.

Seven-One-Two-One. Maintaining the same deep secondary setup, this formation, which is not seen as much since the modern development of the passing game, presents a greater problem to the offense on blocking for running plays due to the extra man on the line of scrimmage.

Goal Line Defenses. When a team gets its back to the wall, in what some sportswriters term the "zone of intense resistance," it can change its defensive alignment because the area to be defended is no longer as big but is much more important. If the offense has first down on the five yard line, the longest pass it can complete is about 14 and ½ yards from the scrimmage line, and the deep pass defense can be moved up to help jam the line. This accounts for the difficulty teams have in ramming through for those last few yards, since the defense packs eight men into the scrimmage line, or might even gamble on more if a pass seems unlikely.

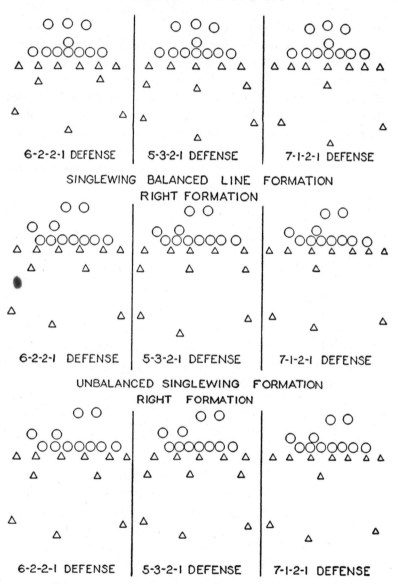

Diagram 31—Basic Defenses Versus Basic Formations

4. Spacing

Such are the standard alignments, but they have many variations. One of the most important of these is in the spacing of the men. The word "spacing" now has a definite meaning in defensive football. It refers to the alignment of the men in the primary line, that is, their position in relation to the men opposite them on offense. There is no such definite way of defining the stationing of the secondary.

When the spacing of a line is balanced, it is called "normal" spacing. This balance depends upon the type of attack it is facing. Diagram 31, page 138, shows normal spacing of the three standard or orthodox alignments against three types of offense; balanced T, balanced Single Wing and unbalanced Single Wing. There are normal spacings against other types of offense, but these will suffice as an example.

The individual linemen have a responsibility, in their defensive charge, to protect themselves from those offensive men who can possibly block them. Diagram 32, this page, shows how this responsibility can be altered by shifting the defensive men half a space. In Part A, each defender can be blocked by one man or blocked two-on-one from either side. This gives them both dual responsibility in their defensive charge to protect themselves from these blocks. As can be seen in the same diagram, there are numerous examples in which normal spacing opens defenders to this dual responsibility.

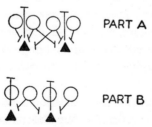

PART A

PART B

Diagram 32—Line Responsibility—Defensive Guard Play

In Part B of the Diagram, the men have been moved half a unit to the left, cutting down the responsibility of the man on the left and assuring the one on the right that there can only be a single block on the defender closest to him if the play comes between them.

Normal spacing, ideally balanced, can be used when one team is much stronger than the other. For practical purposes, however, it is better to realign the spacing in which the defense lines up at the start of a play so that individual responsibility can be lightened as in Diagram B. Although it may not involve movement once the team is lined up, this is called an "overshift" or "undershift" depending on whether it is done toward or away from the strength of the offensive formation. It is in common usage today. Compensation for the line maneuver is usually made by a corresponding shift in the other direction by the linebackers. If the offensive formation is balanced, with no long or strong side, a shift to the wider side of the playing field, toward the direction in which the offense has more room to move, would be an overshift.

Diagram 33 shows a "six-overshift" and "six-undershift" against an unbalanced Single Wing, and a "six-overshift left" against a balanced T.

A close look at the variations of spacing here will show the combinations of spacings of six, seven and five man lines that can result. For instance, the "six-over" against the Single Wing has spacing like that of the seven man line versus the Single Wing on the left side and the five man line on the right side. This is also true in overshifting against the balanced T. Similar shifts of spacing in 5-3-2-1 can achieve six man line spacing on one side and four man line spacing on the other. Shifting a 7-1 can achieve eight man spacing on one side and six on the other.

Along with these spacing variations, now commonly accepted as orthodox, several other defensive stratagems have come into common usage, varying the method of charge.

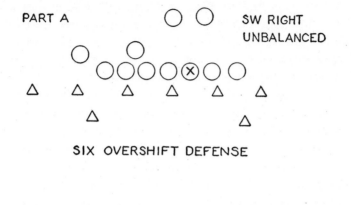

PART A　　　　　　　　　　SW RIGHT
　　　　　　　　　　　　　UNBALANCED

SIX OVERSHIFT DEFENSE

PART B　　　　　　　　　SW RIGHT
　　　　　　　　　　　　UNBALANCE

SIX UNDERSHIFT DEFENSE

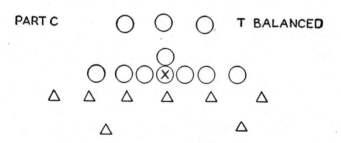

PART C　　　　　　　　T BALANCED

SIX OVERSHIFT LEFT DEFENSE

Diagram 33—Variations in Defensive Spacing

Slant Charge. In this type of charge, the defensive lineman moves obliquely across the line of scrimmage instead of directly ahead.

Loop Charge. Here the lineman moves laterally along the line of scrimmage and then charges straight ahead over a different position.

Both of these are done as team maneuvers with the snap of the ball, in order to achieve the effect of a different spacing at the very last possible second. Slanting is done in the space of about half an offensive position, while looping can be done over the distance of a whole offensive position.

Run-In. Also called a run-through, this is a maneuver in which a linebacker charges into the line at a given point. This has the effect of a last second change of alignment. The gap for the run-in can be left by taking the spacing the run-in will create and leaving the hole there, or it can be cleared by slants or loops away from the spot.

It is unfortunately much easier for the spectator to visualize these various alignments and maneuvers on paper than it is to recognize them on the field. The angle and perspective from which most plays are viewed makes picking them out difficult. A good way of checking them might be to sit behind the goal posts some time, where spacing would be much more clearly visible and understandable. From the sideline, picking out the defensive tackle on the side nearest you and seeing how he lines up in relation to the offensive end opposite him will give you some idea of what kind of spacing the team is using on that play, even though one man cannot indicate the whole pattern, as we have shown.

If you are following our advice, not to watch the ball while a play is in progress, you should be able to pick up information on the kind of charge a defensive team is using. Watch whether the linemen charge straight ahead or make a movement laterally before going in. It is also possible to pick out the development of run-ins through the use of your peripheral vision. The corner of your eye should catch the linebacker charging in just before the snap of the ball.

Even though you are unable to keep abreast of each maneuver by the defense, the knowledge that these exist can help you to understand the problem facing the offense. It should also make you realize that the man making the tackle is following through with what is essentially a team maneuver, with the actions of all eleven men interdependent and complementary.

5. Team Pass Defense

We have discussed the individual skills and traits that a pass defender must have. Now let's relate them to the effort made by the whole team to break up an opponent's passing game.

As we learned from the discussion of the offense, three receivers downfield is generally the best balance for a passing play, which means that pass defense areas are based on the possibility of pass patterns which use these three receivers. Diagram 34, page 144, gives the breakdown of the field into these areas.

The theory behind this diagram is that the three receivers can proceed downfield to catch a pass, limited only by the sidelines, the time the passer has before he has to get rid of the ball, and the strength of his arm. The defense has no way of knowing the pattern to be taken or the moment at which the pass will be thrown, so it must guard against theoretical possibilities.

A shallow defense area can be set up from five to ten yards back of the line of scrimmage. Linebackers can cover this non-expandable area; and the deep area, whose limits are not known, must be defended by the deep secondary trio. With three men deep, the defense has a number equal to the probable number of receivers. Even though a team has only been getting two receivers downfield, the third defender is a good safety factor.

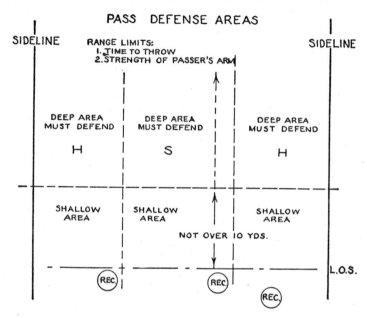

Diagram 34—Pass Defense Areas

Two linebackers cannot cover the three shallow sectors completely, but they can straddle areas in an attempt to give minimum coverage to both and can switch any pattern they follow so that the offense cannot be sure of an advantage.

Changing the alignment to a 5-3-2-1 is, of course, the best method of giving coverage to all the areas on the diagram. When using a 7-1-2-1 in anticipation of a rushing game, passes can be adjusted for by dropping the ends back into the shallow flat, since they are too wide to take part in effective rushing of the passer. In a goal line defense, the pass defense area has been reduced, but the shallow area is doubly important. The deep men must move up to help cover it as well as to provide support for jamming the line.

There are three standard methods of pass defense: zone, man-to-man and combination.

Zone Defense. Here the defenders cover the areas of Diagram 34, page 144, when they see a pass coming, and play to the ball. The deep man has the toughest problem, but he can usually figure that he can meet the ball anywhere it comes into his zone if it is in the air for at least twenty-five yards. The secondary men all watch the passer carefully and react quickly to play the ball in support just the way baseball outfielders do. If no men enter their zone, they ease into an adjoining one to help. In this way they can establish smaller zones within the zones of deep areas.

Man-to-Man. Here the three deep men each pick one of the three potential receivers before the play starts and are responsible for covering him no matter where he goes. They must judge a course that will meet and cover the receiver and use peripheral vision to see the ball coming.

Combination. The two types can be used in conjunction. The defenders are responsible for their zones and then work man-to-man on anyone who comes into it. Defenders with no receivers in their zone must move into a zone that has two receivers and help out.

Pass Rush. A very important part of pass defense is the pass rush. This effort by the primary defense cuts down on the time the passer has to throw and in some cases ends it right there. It can be done as a planned team maneuver when the situation calls for a pass, or it can be spontaneous on the show of a pass.

Throwing the passer for a loss is one of the main objectives of this effort, but in any event the rushing linemen should try to get him off balance before he throws and to destroy his accuracy by getting their hands high over their heads as an obstacle, forcing incompletions and interceptions.

These then are the elements that go into the defensive side of the game. There are other variations that can be used, but, when you run into them, knowledge of the foregoing should enable you to analyze them. Defensive strategy, though it may be impaired by the reduction of coaching time allowed under the return to one platoon, will no more remain static than will the development of offensive formations. Individual coaches will be bound to come up with special defensive strategy for unusual situations.

From the foregoing, you can see that the art of defense is a flexible one, capable of meeting most emergencies. Coaches usually plan their defense in its broader aspect on a seasonal basis, choosing personnel to fit in with long range plans and giving them a general pattern of operation. In slotting personnel on defense, allowance can be made for the fact that most teams are right-handed. No matter how much they try to overcome this, their main strength is to the right, and a team's strongest defenders should be on its left side.

We have now gone into the fundamentals, the terminology and the graphic details of all phases of football. Squad organization and preparation, rules and regulations, and offensive and defensive formations have all been covered.

It is now time to weld them together into an analysis of how a coaching staff uses them in plotting game strategy; and how you can follow the offensive and defensive quarterbacks as they make use of these factors on the field of play.

VIII Plotting Football Strategy

$\mathcal{W}$hen it comes to pre-game strategy, teams and coaches have certain advantages over the spectator, in that they are operating on coordinated game-plans, based on everything they know or "feel" about the opposition. Sometimes game plans are nothing more than intelligent guess work and calculated risks. More often they are products of hours of painstaking work on the part of scouts, coaches, and the players, who are taught the why and wherefore of the particular plan for the day.

The master plan for the strategy to be used against a particular team on a certain day is determined by the amount of accurate information that has been gathered about that opponent. This information can be compiled from many sources. First comes a thorough study of a team's strategy during its past few games with your own team, provided the same head coach remains at the helm. This study should reveal general data on the strengths, weaknesses and preconceptions that are fundamental with that particular team. Past season's movies are of great benefit, but their lessons must be checked again during the current season to learn if there has been a change in the fundamental thinking behind the opponent's offensive and defensive strategy.

That statement brings us to the role and methods of the present day football scouts.

In the past, a scout, or seeker of information about an opposing team, was treated as a spy, which he was. He crept in and out of stadiums or practice fields under a stigma akin to that of a common thief. Today he is an accepted part of the football scheme, for the home team usually provides him with a privileged location high on the sideline or end stands, and he is extended every courtesy. The elevation of this gentleman's "social status" has done much to eliminate suspicion and jealousy among opponents. The scouts are, in most cases, members of the rival coaching staffs although many old lettermen and others interested in football substitute in the role. A new development in scouting, the exchange of motion pictures between staffs during the regular season, is being legalized in some conferences. There are also scouting bureaus or individuals who will disseminate information about individual teams for a price. However, most coaches agree that the best scouts come from members of their own staff because they have a working knowledge of one half of the problem.

The scout's duty is to gather accurate information about an opponent which will simplify coaching during the week of preparation for that opponent. The methods used to assemble these facts about a team may differ with the individuality of the head scout, but the prime purpose remains: acquiring an accurate picture of a team's strength and weakness. Even the great teams of the past have had some "Achilles heels," but the chances are that their opponents lacked the weapons to exploit these weaknesses properly.

The head scout and his helpers divide their attention between both phases of a team's play: offense and defense. In watching a team advance the ball they are seeking answers to certain basic questions.

For instance, what formation or variation of formations does the team favor? How does the personnel fit into the formation? How do individual players change the normal results usually associated with the known strengths of the formation? (Chapter II, on formations, has given you the normal expectancy of strength depending upon where the man are placed in relation to the ball.) How effective is the opponent's kicking, running and passing, and what is the relation of each phase to the whole offensive scheme?

Let us examine what we need to know about their kicking game. This means kick-off, punting, quick kicking and place kicking.

On kick-offs does the ball carry into the end zone or does their kicking average out to a certain yard line? How about height and consistency? Do they kick to the sides or down the center? Effect of the wind? Does the team prefer to kick off? Does it use the short kick, trying for possession? Does it kick from the sides or center of the field? How does it cover kick-offs? Down fast? One side slower than the other? A scout in checking these questions will note the information which is most important to us for our planning.

Punting under the new rules becomes more important than ever, for the specialist cannot be rushed into the game for this important play. Here again we need accurate information which can be utilized.

Does the punter average the normal thirty-five yards from the scrimmage line? Does he take normal steps? Is he slow or fast in kicking? Does he favor right or left? Does he kick high or low? Spiral or end-over-end in flight? How does he react to different wind conditions, to wet weather? Is he well protected by his team? Can he count on accurate passes from his center? A scout notes all pertinent details. He wants to know whether the kick can be blocked or whether we should try to use a planned punt-runback play or defend normally.

The decision about the use of the punt in a team's overall

strategy is most important and we must have answers as to whether kicking is used as an offensive threat or whether it is primarily a defensive play.

The quick kick is definitely an offensive play, as is the regular punt when used on first down. The quick kick comes out of a formation which shows running potential. It is used when the deep defensive man or men are too close to catch the ball, on early downs with favorable wind conditions and also at a stage in the game when possession of the ball is not vital.

The threat of the place kick is reviewed by the scout in conjunction with actual scoring. Primarily he is most concerned about the point after touchdown which is *the* most important single play in the entire game. More games have been decided by this one play than by any other.

As an aside here, a few thoughts might be in order on this controversial play. Should he lose a game by the point after touchdown, a coach's mail bag is more bulging than ever, all over this seemingly simple failure. This would indicate that the average fan does not understand the variables present. In the early days of football the conditions were favorable for a successful kick. As we have already pointed out, the goal posts were on the goal line, and the ball was fat, like a rugby ball, and easier to kick. By using a drop kicker you had one more man as a blocking protector.

If you remember Chapter II, we told how the modern football has been streamlined by the rule makers so that it is now a "passing ball" rather than a "kicking ball," requiring a man as a place kick holder to produce accuracy. The goal posts have been removed from the goal line to prevent injuries and the target is ten yards farther away. The kick now must carry twenty yards, for you will note that the ball is usually placed on the ten yard line. There is one advantage; stop watches have proved that the place kick is faster, thus cutting down the time in which effective protection must be given the kickers. But there are more factors present that can lead to failure.

Aside from the point after touchdown, the threat of a field goal is ever present in a close contest. Our scouts must evaluate that threat when the place kicking formation is used other than for the point after touchdown. Does the team use the formation as a decoy for another type of play, or does it actually try for a field goal if the strategy so dictates?

You now have an inkling of a few of the questions requiring answers before a team's kicking can be evaluated. When you realize that the kick is used in but a small proportion of the total plays per game, you can imagine the details required when a scout examines the potential of a team's running and passing threats. Personnel comes in for close scrutiny, of course, but the main concern is with the strength of each phase of the team's game as demonstrated by game-proven success or failure against various opponents.

The scout can study the game statistics of yards gained or lost by running, passing or kicking, but this is an incomplete story. He needs an individual breakdown if he is to secure the true analysis.

A study of the strength of the running attack would consider the following:

1. Use in proportion to other phases.
2. Use in crucial downs or in sequence calling.
3. Frequency of the use of certain plays in certain zones on the field.

This information would fall into line more readily if the scout could succeed in determining the underlying strategy involved in play selection.

One method of determining a team's running attack is known as the distribution method. A study of the scheme should give the scout certain valuable details. He draws the defensive team's standard line spacing and alignment as played against its opponent's formation (the latter being the team he is scouting). Between the defensive positions he can now make a record of the FREQUENCY with which the team strikes at certain sectors and can record the percentage of SUCCESS which comes to it in that area. A simple chart, Diagram 35, will help on this problem. The positions given are those of a defensive line as the offense looks at it. Suppose a first quarter history of the running attack of the team being scouted is studied. For our own defensive planning we can then use the average per play to deduce the following about that team:

1. Running strength is to the right.
2. It is more dangerous around end and between guards than elsewhere.
3. It is abnormally weak to the left.
4. Our defensive men must be placed to stop this unbalance in the attack.

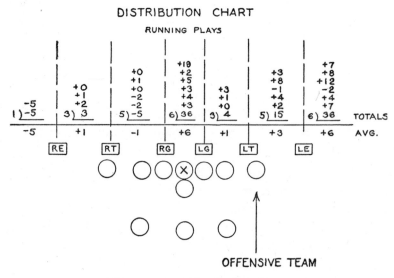

Diagram 35—Distribution Chart

When judging a team's offensive running potential, we must study the defensive spacing and quality of personnel it has met, plus the personnel variables of its own defense. Only then can we make a decision as to just where we can over-balance to stop this threat.

The potency of the passing attack of the team under scouting observation is analyzed in the same manner, to ascertain the following:

1. Its pass threat as a ground gainer or scoring weapon.
2. The reliance a team places on passing and the frequency of use.
3. Success of passes in certain areas, to certain receivers and in certain situations.
4. The passer himself, his accuracy, ability to deceive and reaction under pressure in the form of a heavily rushing defense.

When our scout has all this information, he then studies the strategy of the team as evidenced by the quarterback's play selections from game to game. Some cue toward how he blends the running and passing attack can be obtained from a study of plays used in different downs and yardage sequences.

A careful history of all plays called on first, second and third downs, with the yardage then needed for a first down, will reveal helpful information. More important, we would like information on the play selection when his team comes up to a crucial down,* or when it faces a close defeat with the clock running out. Another vital indication is the play called when a team receives the ball on an unexpected break.

Our scout is ever alert for personal mannerisms which give away the direction or type of play. However, the defense cannot place too much faith in diagnosing a pass as a result

---

* A crucial down is one that presents the last chance to gain yardage before a team is forced to surrender the ball by a punt or on downs.

of the passer licking his fingers, a running play because a ball carrier hitches his pants or a kick because a kicker cleans his cleats. Coaches are ever watchful for giveaway mannerisms like these in practice sessions. Players are warned and the results checked by game movies. Modern football teams, scouted by impartial observers, are far beyond this elementary sort of vulnerability. Successful defensive plans have been predicated upon mannerisms in the past, where certain players gave away the type of play, permitting an all out defense against its type. Such plans can backfire, though, if the offense uses the telltale movement as an intentional false lead on a crucial down.

Offensive planning from scouting reports follows the same procedure as defensive planning, with the thinking naturally reversed. We can again use the chart on page 152, this time as applying to the defense of the team being scouted. Revealing as it does the amount of territory our next opponent has yielded when plays are directed at his left side, the chart indicates a vulnerability of running plays there. This weakness may be the result of poor personnel or type of alignment. In either event, it would be wise to concentrate early runs against that sector until a change by the defense proves it unwise. Our quarterback would be advised to test the guard area, too, because the percentage of yards per play is above normal there.

Our scout watches especially for individual weakness in separate positions: ends who defend better outside their position than inside, tackles who can be trapped rather than powered, guards who drift rather than hold position. He watches to see whether linebackers crash to the heart of a play or exchange defensive responsibilities with linemen in their area. He is ever alert to the play of the defensive halfbacks. Do they support the ends to the outside or inside? Do they cover well when plays are run away from them? What are the safety man's movements? Does he support the line, or is he the last line of defense? All the answers tell the staff something about the opponent's defensive ideas.

After a thorough study of individual characteristics, all positions are now evaluated in respect to each other. This gives our quarterback a chance to start a game knowing he faces weak ends, strong tackles and, say, average guards.

The use of the forward pass as a scoring weapon has become the greatest threat to the defense, with increased emphasis on passing attacks in all sectors of the country. Our scout will use every resource to find out the pass defense coverage of an opponent, not only by team scheme, but also on the separate duties of line and backs. It is generally conceded in the coaching fraternity that there is no bullet-proof pass defense against all types of pass patterns that can be thrown from varied formations. Finding what loopholes are left open is the scout's job.

If we cannot discover the general passing coverage system of a team, we are eager to learn of any individual weakness which might give us an advantage. Does a certain back cover better to his outside than inside his position? Is he weak on long passes behind him, short hooks in front or delayed passes into his area?

Accurate answers to such questions govern our pre-game plans, with no important detail overlooked. Practice during the week would tend to stress maneuvers to be used Saturday so as to sharpen our attacking weapons and strengthen our defenses where we expect the opponent's major assault.

It is not beyond the more experienced fan's capability to analyze his own team in this way too. He could begin to understand the problems of the coaching staff as they endeavor to strengthen apparent weaknesses from week to week. He could follow the records and even learn something about the potential of the opposition. He might figure out the pregame strategy of the two teams, but would only be guessing unless he were able to attend their practice sessions. Sportswriters, who enjoy the confidence of the coaches and use what they see strictly for their own guidance in watching a game, are often able to interpret Saturday's battle for you more thoroughly and accurately through having attended practice sessions at both camps.

With the technical information at hand accurately compiled and evaluated, our staff is now ready for working out the pre-game strategy. It is seeking the surest, safest method of matching strength with strength on both offense and defense, with one idea foremost—to win, by every legitimate maneuver sanctioned by the rules and code of ethics.

All pre-game strategy will be subject to review the day of the game. Weather conditions can upset the apple cart. Strong winds are important. Snow, rain, abnormal hot or cold temperatures or any combination of these elements, together with ground and turf conditions, all have an important bearing on the conduct of the game. If you come to the game early, you will see the opposing staffs checking weather conditions in time for pre-game instructions to their teams.

It must be remembered that any or all pre-game strategy may have to be abandoned after the events of the first half, no matter what the weather. Sometimes a surprise defense or offense by the opposition dictates entirely new methods from those worked out from the scouting report. The ability of a team to react to such unforeseen tactics will mark it as an experienced or a green team. A team should also be prepared for a sudden change in the opponent's tactics at the start of the second half, for some coaches do not show their hands until that time. They prefer to hide their intentions until after the halftime intermission so that adjustments will be more difficult. Now that platoons cannot go in and out of the game on each change of ball, this is even more advantageous.

It is time now to take you down on the field for the final pre-game preparation. Every move is planned in detail whether the game is at home or away. The pre-game warm-up follows a set routine: so many minutes for kicking, so many for passing, so many for ball handling, the purpose being to prepare the team for play under the actual conditions of the moment. Pre-game instructions in the locker room consist of a reminder on the important points in a strategy already worked out.

Between the halves there is also an established routine. The twelve minutes start with a five minute physical check by the team physician and trainers, while the players are resting in pre-determined places. The head coach and spotters are meanwhile consulting on possible second half adjustments in over-all strategy, or a change from the details of first half offensive and defensive assignments. The last seven minutes are used to solidify any new plans or to stress the original plans if they were not used properly in the first half and still seem advantageous.

The former custom of impassioned oratory by old grads is definitely out. Modern football demands full mental concentration for execution of the many details involved. Emotional tirades or upsetting incidents tend to destroy the poise needed for performing at peak efficiency.

It is true that the mental attitude before and during games has won and lost more battles than any other single factor, but only those close to the team in an official capacity are in a position to judge the proper approach for any particular game.

Experienced coaches are past masters in the psychological warfare which precedes a season or a traditional game. Some of the statements issued are for public consumption, some are in hopes that the mental attitude of the players will be beneficially affected as game time nears. As for dressing room oratory by the coach, that is a matter of individual character and choice, not subject to generalization, though it is safe to say that the art is on the decline.

In football's propaganda wars, you often hear of coaches known for their use of the proverbial "crying towel." Without condemning or condoning individuals, it seems unfair to let the subject pass without a plea in behalf of a profession which must operate in a glare of pitiless publicity and under circumstances in which one unlucky bounce of a ball or the uncertainties of the human factor in teen-age youngsters can bring complete disaster to well laid plans.

Very often alumni are howling quite unfairly, and even college administrations are demanding victory week by week. Can a coach be blamed if he protects himself with a little public wringing of that towel? Wouldn't it be fairer to judge him on how he organizes his job and follows it through than on the bare won-lost record? Only half the coaches can win on any given Saturday, and we have tried to outline here some of the standards, other than victory, by which a coaching staff can be judged.

IX Calling Them with the Quarterbacks

$\mathcal{I}$n the opening ceremony of the game, the toss of the coin for choice of goals gives the lucky captain the opportunity to make his first strategic decision. The captain who wins the toss can elect to kick off, or to receive or defend either goal. The opposing captain, on losing the toss, can now counter with the alternate choice, which may have been his original choice had he won. This ceremony takes place either just before the game, or, in a new option starting with the 1953 rules, half an hour before game time to allow the teams a longer period to solidify pre-game plans.

With the weather of negligible consequence, the decision to kick off or receive is usually governed by the estimated strength of the two teams, or by the presence of a fine kick-off man who can kick the ball over the goal line. This creates an automatic touchback if downed by the receiving team behind the goal, and starts that team out at a theoretical disadvantage, as kickoff returns average out to the thirty-two yard line.

The pre-game strategy, discussed in the previous chapter, has been decided long before the actual tossing of the coin. Usually the coach, captain and offensive and defensive quarterbacks confer on the way the game is to be played, taking into consideration the alternate choices depending on the call of the coin.

Football games start exactly on time, for there is a fifteen yard penalty if a team is late. During the warm-up period, the Field Judge, who is the official timer, coordinates his watch with both coaches, who are responsible for the prompt arrival of their teams. The captains must appear on the sidelines three minutes before scheduled kickoff time. You will note that the four officials, after inspecting the field and playing equipment, will meet five minutes before starting time, two on each side of the field. On a pre-arranged signal, they escort the opposing captains to the exact center of the field, where introductions are made.

The Referee, who is the chief official, will turn to the visiting captain to request a call of the coin as the traditional silver dollar spins high above their heads.

If you have arrived on time and checked the wind and sun, see how you would call the choice of goal if you were the lucky captain. If weather conditions are a negligible factor, how would you guess the choice on pre-game knowledge of the teams? Now watch the referee for the answer. He will usually place his arm on the shoulder of the winner and point to the choice of goal, or designate by hand or feet signals if the choice is to kick off or receive.

Observe where the ball is placed on the kicking team's 40 yard line between the "hash marks" referred to in Chapter IV. Remember they divide the 52-yard-wide field into equal thirds. Has the kicker placed his tee as near the sidelines as possible? If so, he plans to kick for depth straight down the sidelines to limit the runback to the closed side of the field, or diagonally across the field so that his fastest men can arrive simultaneously with the descent of the ball. If he chooses the exact center of the field, he may attempt to kick deep in the end zone. Kicking from the center of the field toward the corners is dangerous because of the rule which gives the ball to the receiving team on its own 40 yard line after two such out-of-bounds kicks.

If the kicker places the ball on the ground or on its side on the tee, he no doubt intends to top the ball along the ground or give it an unnatural spin so that the receivers will find it difficult to handle. He may even try to kick the ball into the five men on the receiving team who, by rule, must be within the 45 yard line zone, hoping for a fumble by these inexperienced ball handlers and a recovery by his own team. An important point to remember is that the ball must travel 10 yards beyond the kicker before his own team can recover it, nor can the ball be recovered before it has touched the ground. Aside from these conditions, however, the kickoff is a free ball and the kicking team can gain possession of it, even in the other team's end zone. This is one of the cheapest touchdowns possible, and one of the most demoralizing for the receivers, but it has been known to happen.

Short kickoffs are employed by teams as a surprise move at the start of the game, or late in the first half or final period, in situations where possession of the ball is extremely important.

In any event, the kicking team should avoid a kickoff that goes high down the middle to the 10 yard line. This allows the receiving team to block the tacklers on a prearranged play and presents it with a golden opportunity to score on that spectacular favorite of the fans, the long runback.

The ball has been kicked off. The receiving team has returned the ball to the neutral position on the field, averaged out in theory as its own 32 yard line. The pre-game planning and strategy will soon be in evidence.

THE QUARTERBACKS

The mental duel between the offensive and defensive quarterbacks can be compared to the physical duel between two highly trained pugilists. The precise method of winning the contest hinges on the pre-game strategy, but you should remember that this strategy may be completely altered because of an unforseeable "break." Most frequent errors, called "breaks," are a fumble of the kickoff, first punt or on the first running play; a penalty requiring an early punt or causing a big yardage deficit in a down sequence; an error in judgment in fielding a punt or kickoff; a punt striking your own team before touching the ground, or even easing over the sideline very close to the goal line in that deadly "coffin corner."

Let's go into the strategy of the opening quarter here. In the absence of one of these breaks early in the game, normal procedure calls for using the pre-game plans. Shall we gamble quickly for an easy touchdown, indicated by a study of scouting data that has revealed such a gamble as within reason? Or shall we stick to trusting the solidity of our team and start the contest in the normal fashion, using basic plays to test the defenses usually favored by the enemy?

The quick-scoring, easy touchdown gamble may not be such a wild chance as it seems, provided the scouting evidence reveals a glaring weakness. This could be owing to poor personnel or an opportunity to exploit a player's carelessness. If successful, such a move could turn an otherwise close contest into a rout, though mental attitude and team morale can be factors in preventing such a calamity. If the opposition does not crack under this early surprise, the contest could resume its normal course. However, the quick score could still be *the* one which decides the game.

In modern football there are two quarterbacks, one to call signals for offense and one to call signals for the defense.

Each has his full complement of strategic material in the form of prearranged plays. These can be utilized for both normal and abnormal situations which may arise.

OFFENSIVE QUARTERBACKS

In a previous book, "Modern Single Wing Football," I made the following statement, which is still pertinent and bears repeating.

Before discussing the technicalities of a modern quarterback's duties, may I extend to him my greatest salute of respect. His problems and responsibilities are more important than those of any man in any other position. The quarterback has always been the coach on the field since the day he was given this authority. He controls the movements of ten other men, directing their offensive destinies for the entire time his team has the ball, and in addition must be proficient in all his own personal assignments.

The current stress on defense, which presents a changing problem from one series of downs to the next, or even within one series, would drive an individual without the determination a quarterback must have to frustrated and haphazard decisions. There was a day when a quarterback could presume a somewhat standard defensive alignment and spacing, depending upon the formation from which he normally started his offense. All that peace of mind is a thing of the past. No longer can he anticipate the usual defenses. He must be mentally prepared to expect the abnormal and be ready to take advantage of opportunities presented by the new theory of team defensive stratagems.

It is now time to examine that statement in detail. In order to recognize the quarterback's problem, we must place ourselves in his position.

What are the fundamental qualifications needed for a field general before he takes up actual training in play calling, and before he is tested under fire in actual game conditions? Primarily he must be a leader who can sell himself to his teammates by his coolness and ability to think clearly under any and all game conditions. He must command their complete confidence and respect in times of deep adversity. He must have a thorough technical knowledge of *every* play at his command, its design, its purpose, and just why such a play has been included in the attack. He must have a thorough knowledge of the strengths and weaknesses of his own teammates. He must know the basic theory behind the attacking formations if he carries more than once. If only one, then he should be versed in the variations of that formation and just how these variations are to be used. He must have a gambler's confidence and the sense to turn conservative at the right time. He must be a complete extrovert but still cautious when strategy so dictates. He must have the instinct for calling his plays so as to win the game by the safest method, with a flexibility that can turn to boldness when the situation calls for it. He must never allow the opposing defensive quarterback to type his play calling. He should vary his calls on crucial downs just enough to confuse the defensive quarterback and still not jeopardize his team's strategic position. He must be a youngster who will gladly accept responsibility, will take the blame for failure even when he is not the cause. He must be an optimist under the most discouraging conditions.

Do such paragons exist? They do, but such a lad is rare indeed, and fortunate is the coach who can find one on his squad. The qualifications are so high that the coach looks primarily for the individual, disregarding the position he plays. Custom and expediency will see to it that he finds his way into the backfield. Here the field general is in a better position to diagnose defensive formations and personnel, but there is no hard and fast rule about where he must play.

In modern football the offensive quarterback gives his play selections in the huddle. This method of conveying the play has become almost universal. In the past, numerical signals were called while the team was aligned in formation. A recent innovation has been the adoption of the open huddle, in which the quarterback faces his men, who in turn are stationed 8-10 yards deep, facing the opposition.

Two factors make huddles an improvement over the old method of calling signals. They allow simpler signals, which would be decipherable if called openly, and prevent the noise of large crowds in a stadium from causing confusion and misunderstanding.

The quarterback enters the huddle, give a simple number, like "42," which may be an end run; or he may have a name for the play, such as "right end sweep." He then gives the number on which the ball is to be snapped, before "hiking" the team into formation. There must be no confusion in the huddle, for a team cannot be successful if all ten men try to advise the quarterback on his play choice.

The quarterback must be willing, however, to accept advice from teammates in whom he has confidence. He must know when and how to use such information and how to remain the boss while taking it. He must know that "too many cooks spoil the broth." A team can function with only *one* quarterback on offense and one on defense, both players who are trained by the coaching staff for that exacting assignment.

With the above in mind, how can we, as individual spectators, have the temerity to criticize a youngster whose thinking may have been perfect on a certain play only to have a mechanical breakdown—a missed block or assignment, or a dropped pass or fumble—nullify his decision? The rules state that a play must be selected and in execution within 25 seconds after the referee leaves the ball. Within this time, the quarterback must take all factors into consideration and pick the play in the face of all the possible uncertainties. Second guessers then cheer when it works and invariably claim that it was their choice too. When it fails to work, they blame the quarterback for his stupidity.

Is it any wonder then that I repeat that the men behind the scenes have complete and sympathetic understanding of the field general's problems? We admire the courage of the boy who will accept this great responsibility.

The offensive quarterback can plan to win the game by utilizing his team's inherent strength in the three phases of offensive football, kicking, running and passing. The superiority of any one of these three phases is determined by his personnel or the stress each phase has received from the coaching staff.

To win by kicking, he must have a superior punter, strong coverage of punts to protect the yardage gained by kicking and a far superior defensive team to hold on to the advantage once it has been gained. Thus the kicking team can be assured early and frequent possession of the ball, allowing it to kick often, even on the first down of a series. Wet weather often brings this strategy to the fore.

To win the game with a running attack, a team must be equipped with a number of well-designed running plays combining power and deception, with enough passing strength to prevent the defense from packing or overloading to stop the runs. The plays must be typed as long-gain gambles or short sure-gainers. They may also be catalogued as plays for position on the field and as situation plays in relation to down, yardage, score and the state of the clock. Plays are usually designed in sequence or in series in the formation. This means that certain plays complement each other because they start alike. The ball is received by the same player, who in turn executes the same backfield maneuver of spinning, faking or whatever. However, the play eventually meets the defense at different speeds and at different defensive sectors. The series should include both inside and outside plays; i.e., inside or outside the defensive tackles. A field general will want to balance the calls between the inside and outside attack, anticipating a longer but less certain gain on the outside plays.

When the quarterback features the passing game, he will know that the emphasis differs from the ground attack strategy as suggested above. When dependence is placed on passing to win games, a team must carry the maximum number of passing plays that can be properly learned.

Practice during the week will stress the actual throwing and receiving of passes by the players who will work together in the games. All types of passes: hooks, crosses, drags, personals, choices, etc., must be mastered. The passing attack must be complemented by a series of plays known as "pass checks," plays that start like pass plays but develop into running plays. The design of this type of play falls into a separate category and differs from the plays in a running sequence in that the play takes advantage of a defense that is overbalanced in expectation of passes. Such plays are known as fake-pass-and-runs. They are directed around the ends or go up between the six or five defensive linemen.

Defensive overbalance in rushing the passer can be exploited by using screen passes, short passes thrown into the flank and center areas over the heads of defensive linemen and linebackers who are allowed deep penetration in rushing the passer. Additional plays are designed to outguess a defense which has been schooled to prevent the best receivers from reaching their usual receiving areas. These plays are usually power plays, aimed at the defensive man who holds up the receiver from breaking downfield.

Quarterbacking the passing attack calls for the same ingenuity as that required to run a ground attack. The point to remember is that the selection of plays in sequence differs from the running attack because of the different method chosen to advance the ball.

This simple chart (Diagram 36) of the field may help to describe some of the quarterback's problems. If his team has the ball in Zone A, he must be conservative and kick the ball out of danger. The closer he is to his own goal, the sooner the ball should be punted. Zone B might be called the experimental zone where the opponent's defenses and defensive thinking can be tested, stressing the running attack. Zone C might be known as the offensive zone, where full exploitation of the running and passing attacks can take place. Zone D is the scoring zone. Here the quarterback decides whether his team can run the ball over by basic plays, or whether he must rely on special scoring plays.

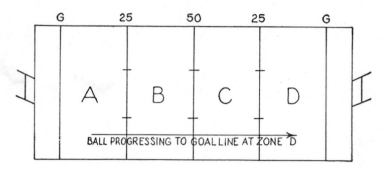

Diagram 36—Field Zone Chart

Possession of the ball is all-important to the offensive quarterback, and he must select plays which will insure his team having the maximum number of opportunities for putting the ball in play. The rule requiring that 10 yards be gained on four downs is the one which most often determines his selection of plays. The chart on the zones will be a factor in his choice.

Here are the variables he must consider. If he is conservative in a zone near his goal line, the play chosen should have the possibility of a large gain with a minimum risk of losing the ball by a fumble—therefore one with a minimum of ball handling. If the quarterback decides he is going to have to kick on third down when he starts calling in a first-down-and-ten-yards-to-go situation, he must plan to gain 10 yards in two tries. Suppose he selects a play whose average gain, as worked out in the detailed play analyses we have already mentioned, has been five yards. The off-tackle play, which is sound and not a gamble, is an example. Two such successive plays could be ones outside each defensive tackle. The probable gain of 10 yards would advance the ball into a zone where it would be safe to kick on fourth down. The quarterback now can select three instead of two plays with the objective of gaining the 10 yards.

Suppose, however, instead of gaining five yards on the first play in the earlier sequence, he gains two yards. The situation is second-and-eight on the next play. What now? A play which might lose that two or could possibly gain the eight? Or should he kick on second down because of the improbability of gaining eight yards on one play? Or should he gamble on a short pass that looks like a run, remembering that he might lose the ball on an interception.

Let's suppose that on the first-and-ten call the quarterback gained eight yards instead of the average five. Does he now choose a sure two yard play or does he call a play that starts as a two yard play trying to decoy the defense so that he can gain 20 or 30 yards by surprise?

Designating the position of the ball on the field by arbitrary zones and taking into account the position of the ball laterally in such zones can aid materially in the choice of play that fits the problem of down and distance to be gained. Almost all coaches use elastic zones for teaching new quarterbacks the fundamentals behind sound signal calling.

The quarterback who knows when to abandon the pattern of orthodox calling is usually the one most feared by the defense, particularly one who strikes quickly for a score when an unexpected opportunity presents itself. For example, if in midfield a team should gain nine yards on the first-and-ten call, the defensive quarterback has an almost impossible situation in trying to recover the ball in that sequence, since the offensive team has two or three tries to make the one yard. The offensive quarterback now has a free choice for a gamble on a long gain play which, if the play does not change his position, still leaves him in a situation of third down, one to go, an easy assignment in two tries.

It is imperative that the quarterback consider the time left to play, particularly near the end of the quarters, half or the game itself. Some plays by their nature consume more time than others. Certain plays which end up out of bounds or as incomplete passes stop the clock. These are an advantage or disadvantage depending on whether you are ahead or behind and want to get in as many plays as possible or run out the clock to keep the ball away from the opposition.

Hundreds of games are decided each Saturday by the quarterback who knows the proper method of using the time-left-to-play factor to his team's advantage. At your next game, try to recognize the reason why a decision has been made and just how it was carried out.

It is also important that a quarterback keep his team as near as possible to the center of the field laterally so that the defense cannot use the sideline to limit his choice of plays and direction.

He must have a thorough knowledge of spacing. In Chapter VII we pointed out that the standard alignments, such as 6-2-2-1, can be altered by the spacing of the men on the primary line. There may be six men on the line of scrimmage, but their exact positions can in effect create five or seven man line situations in certain areas. The quarterback must find out from his linemen not only where the opponents take their original position in this spacing, but also whether they charge hard and straight ahead, angle hard right or left with the slant charge, loop around offensive men, use a soft charge, or stand still. He must know if the defensive men charge and expose their territory for running plays that cannot be recognized from their original position in lining up. He must know the position of the linebackers, who may number from one to four and may be using run-ins to change the spacing. Where are they spaced? What are their defensive duties in conjunction with the men on the defensive line? How deep are the halfbacks? Do they cover inside or outside the defensive ends? Do they react slowly to runs, or do they come up too fast? Where does the safety man play? What are his duties against runs, kicks and passes?

When the quarterback can type a team's defensive plans he has a distinct advantage in his play calling. If he can anticipate a standard defense against a certain situation, for example the same defensive alignment and type of line charge against a first-and-ten situation in the same zone of the field, play calling can become a happy and rewarding experience.

If the field general cannot type the defensive scheme of the opposition, he must rely on sequence calling, such as the following example: if a play outside tackle is stopped, he might try running inside that position. If the defensive end floats wide to prevent encircling movement, he might try a play that runs inside that end. If the halfback comes up quickly to stop the off-tackle play on the line of scrimmage, he might select a play that looks like the off-tackle run at its inception but becomes a deep pass behind the halfback's position.

A discerning quarterback can learn about defensive play of individuals if he checks the identity of the tackler on each play. A complete knowledge of his own team's assignments will tell him whether the blocking failed to take the designated man, or if the defensive player is in a position where he cannot be blocked by the man assigned.

When no flagrant weakness appears in the opposition, the wise strategy is to play a conservative game. Realizing that basic plays are the heart of any attack, the field general should start his campaign by ascertaining if the opponents have geared their defenses to stop his best assets, either plays or players. This does not necessarily mean that runs will be stressed over passes or vice versa. To achieve this purpose he will employ basic plays considered by the coaching staff as solid in the overall attack. If early success reveals a weakness that calls for a repeat of the basic plays, our quarterback's problems again become simplified. Steady gains will eventually cause a basic defense to become stretched to stop these plays, giving opportunities that otherwise would never appear. If the "basics" are held in check either by an overbalanced defense or one that is clever in design, appearing weak in spots but in reality overbalanced in that sector, then the perplexed pilot might well consider the checks and balances which complement the basics and are available for such an emergency.

Remember that the depth and width of the relative positions of the ball carriers before the snap of the ball, regardless of the name of the formation, gives the alignment certain strengths and weaknesses. Player personnel and abilities may change these factors slightly, but not radically. If the defensive quarterback has been forced to alter his basic defenses to check the basic plays or key players, the strategy calls for a trial of the "semi-basics," which may now hold more potential than the old standbys. Success here may further overbalance a basic defense, allowing a wide-open long-gain play that decides the contest.

Thus the analogy is that of the boxer, who, while holding his Sunday punch, feints and spars for an opening. If by clever tactics the quarterback's method reveals a glaring weakness in the kicking, running or passing defenses, the wise campaigner then maneuvers skillfully. As the field general senses that the time is right, the big punch, in the form of a quick kick on a surprise down, a specially designed pass disguised as a basic run, or a long-gain running play, can be the decisive blow to an opponent's hope for supremacy.

Defensive Quarterbacks

Now that you have been briefed about the offensive quarterback and his problems, let's execute a complete switch in our thinking to learn about the quarterback who calls the defensive signals. You will note, incidentally, that the term quarterback has lost all identification with position and has come to mean a signal caller, whether on offense or defense.

This defensive quarterback must have mental qualifications to match those of the offensive signal caller. He is usually stationed as one of the linebackers. From this position, he can observe the backfield maneuvers and the possible giveaways that will help him call his plays. In describing the qualifications for playing on defense, we have already said that the linebacker should be one of the soundest football players on the squad because of the requirements of the position. This is another reason for the common assignment of defensive quarterback duties to one of these men.

The plays that a defensive quarterback calls designate the type of alignment to be taken and the type of spacing to go with it, along with any special tactics such as looping and slanting by the line as described in Chapter VII. Last second changes by dropping a man in or out of the scrimmage line are also used.

The gradual evolution of defense has made the defensive quarterback just as important to team victory as his counterpart on offense. Rule developments giving the offense an edge have forced coaching staffs to devote more time to defense if they expect their teams to regain possession of the ball. Individual and team defensive play being more natural and instinctive, as we have pointed out, the general rule among coaches has been to allot from thirty to thirty-five per cent of the practice time for team-defensive coaching.

Two platoon football allowed full practice time to be devoted to defense and this resulted in a large number of defensive plays being available for choice by the signal caller. Changes in coaching methods after the 1953 rule change mean less time to teach these plays, but their possibility still exists for they are now a part of the accepted practices of the game.

Generally the defense must carry plays that overbalance the

team defense, with the object of matching strength with strength when an opponent's offense reveals overbalance in some phase of the game, such as kicking, running or passing. To offset the opponents' strength in kicking, the defensive quarterback must have plays to hurry the kicker and offset his accuracy. These are in the nature of punt-blocking plays that are planned with a rush at the kicker from either flank or the center area. Defensive superiority in punt-rushing plays sometimes results in blocked punts. The blocked punt can be one of the most valuable plays in the game because of the lowered morale of the victimized team. The man who blocks the kick gets his name in the paper and all the cheers, but remember the next time you see this "break" that it was very likely brought about by the combined efforts of most of the defensive team in a specific and well-executed play. When an offensive team is lined up for a punt, use your peripheral vision to watch the actions of the defense and you may pick up the execution of this play at its inception.

In order to overbalance the team defense so as to stop a strong running attack, the quarterback must have enough leeway to allow him to place sufficient men on the line of scrimmage to stop this type of attack at its inception. Eight man defensive lines and variations of the six and seven man defensive lines are commonly used. The use of secondary to support the defensive line at close range varies with the strength of the running attack being faced. Two and sometimes three men are needed to support the line, especially when the goal is threatened at close range. Overbalanced strength against runs will leave the defense open to passing and kicking, but a team's defense must be flexible enough so that it can be quarterbacked to meet any overbalanced strength of the offense.

If the defensive quarterback finds that he can use fewer men on the line of scrimmage, his overall defense becomes more balanced and therefore better adapted to take care of a sudden change in the offensive team's plans. Defensive pressure against running plays can be gradually lessened by dropping from an 8-3 alignment to a 7-4, 6-3 or 6-2, creating a better balance to stop both runs and passes. While watching a game, see if you can keep ahead of the defensive signal caller on these switches by recognizing the situation he faces.

To overbalance a team defense against a passing attack, the regular defenses would deploy less men on the line of scrimmage if the pass patterns were of the short or medium variety, but would use more men to rush the passer if the passes were of abnormal length. Generally five men on the line of scrimmage is a desirable number, since the extra linebacker is needed to help cover additional receivers or an open zone. A sudden change to a 5-3 defense may mean the defensive team is looking for a pass, particularly if there is large yardage to be gained on a late down, for example a third-and-twelve situation. A 5-4 defense would mean that men are needed in the short or flat areas to stop the threat of a completion there.

Another defensive stratagem which helps to neutralize the passing game is an overbalanced pass rush, either on flanks or up the middle. The principal objective of the overbalanced defense against the passing game is to rush the receiver hard enough to impair his accuracy, hoping for an interception and score. Some teams also use delaying tactics against an offense's favorite receiver, particularly if such a receiver is especially dangerous. Thus, the defensive quarterback has a number of ways to concentrate against a strong passing game, although it is practically impossible to prevent pass completions by an excellent passer, afforded good protection, to outstanding receivers.

A team also always carries some special defenses for use against special plays they know they may meet, or to handle an outstanding player of extraordinary ability, but these are not important in an understanding of the basic defensive strategy. This overall strategy should be to regain the ball

for the offense, but to try to score while the opponents have
the ball, if possible.

The defensive quarterback's calls are governed by the identical factors considered by an offensive signal caller: the clock,
stage of the game, score, weather, and the offensive plans of
his own team. Since the strategic thinking of the offensive
quarterback varies in the different zones of the field, the defensive quarterback must try to guess the choice of play, overbalance his defensive alignment to stop the play for no gain
and create a situation that will allow him greater freedom in
calling the next series of defensive plays.

As an illustration, when the situation is first-and-ten, no
score, and the ball in a neutral position around the offense's 32
yard line, the balance between offense and defense is even.
If the offensive quarterback is in a gambling mood, he may
try a long gaining play in this situation. If the gamble fails,
leaving the offensive quarterback with a second-and-ten situation, the defensive quarterback can now call defensive plays
that will allow a greater defensive leeway as the down approaches when a punt must be called for to transfer possession
of the ball.

The defensive quarterback may overbalance his defenses in
a certain zone to create the situation above, that is, second-
and-ten. His call, not the failure of the offensive gamble,
places him in a favorable situation.

Let's assume that the gamble of the offensive quarterback
succeeds, making the situation second-and-two. The defensive
quarterback is now in a dilemma. Should he try to prevent
the opponents from gaining the two yards by overbalancing
his defense against the most obvious move, or would it be
safer to "give" the offensive team the two yards by keeping
a balanced defense, so that the defensive quarterback has a
more equitable situation to meet in the next series of downs?

The latter choice may be wise toward the end of the half
when the defensive team has the opponents deep in their own

territory. The strategy now calls for the defense to allow the other team to gain ground but to contain the gains short of a score, provided of course further possession of the ball is not necessary to the defensive team. Therefore, when you see a team yielding yardage to run the clock out, it is probably calculated strategy, rather than a sudden breakdown of hitherto stubborn defenses, like a boxer who knows he has won on points and decides to "coast" in the late rounds and concentrate on avoiding a knockout.

These are the problems a defensive quarterback must weigh between spurts of rugged physical contact while he plays a big part in making his strategy work by doing some tackling. Watch the signals being made, usually by hand signals while the player is on his side of the scrimmage line with his back to the opposition. He may occasionally call a defensive huddle. If need be, the close secondary can relay the signals to the deep men if they are too far back to pick them up.

And so we can see that this matching of wits, the mental side of the football contest, is continual, with a thousand "ifs" "ands" and "buts" to influence each other in an interlocking stream of events.

When unlimited substitution was prevalent, many coaches used to substitute between plays, thereby relieving the individual quarterbacks of this tremendous responsibility, but basic quarterbacking rules are not difficult to learn. Most fall into the category of "don'ts," which, in the past, when violated, have brought on defeat. "Don't pass with a six point lead late in the game" is an example. Most are based on commonsense principles that allow the quarterback to advance the ball with the greatest security.

It is my personal belief that the most successful quarterbacks are those who, once schooled in the psychological aspects of their duties and then given experience under actual game conditions, are eventually allowed to make the final decisions on the field. Coaches on the sideline do not have the complete picture existing on the field of play, and the time factor may prevent their taking advantage of sudden opportunities. Also, a player, though he has inevitably made mistakes during his early training, is in the long run able to become a finer quarterback when he is able to draw on those failures in achieving future successes.

Modern football procedure during games makes full use of the telephone from spotters placed high in the stadium in order to get a clearer picture of the positions of the players. Some teams use squads of spotters on the sides and ends of the field with connecting telephones to the bench, where the head coach has the worst seat in the stadium. Their purpose is to aid the quarterback in selecting his plays, since the spotters are continually checking possible openings for successful plays all during the game. Many games have been won or lost because of the efficiency of the spotters, coach and quarterback. You in your seat high in the stadium or in front of a television may be able to spot weaknesses or situations that are exploitable. Of course, sometimes it is not expedient to strike for victory at once. However, if the opportunity is apparent to you as a spectator, the odds are favorable for its early utilization by the quarterback. Remember that exact spacing in the defensive line is most important, along with the deployment of the secondary in respect to each other and in depth.

With your knowledge of what certain offensive and defensive formations should indicate, according to the state of the game, see if you can anticipate some of the offensive and defensive calls while watching a game. Put yourself into the situation, look for the details that should be significant, and your participation in an afternoon of football should be greatly enriched. You can enjoy the mental side of a football contest, the challenge of the strategy, long after you are no longer able to take the physical bumps of blocking and tackling.

X *The Sunday Paper*

$\mathcal{Y}$our ability to analyze football for your own enjoyment need not stop with the actual viewing of the game. While a coach might seem to have enough troubles without advocating any more "Monday Morning Quarterbacks," there can be no denying that Sunday newspaper accounts of games, along with some of the midweek interviews and practice stories, can provide valuable data for evaluating your own team and its future opponents.

To do this you must be able to use the information properly. One of the favorite indoor sports of some football fans is to follow through with comparative scores in an attempt to rate teams. This has been proven a completely useless pursuit for anything but gags. Each season it is possible to use comparative scores to prove that Podunk Teachers Jayvees could beat the nation's number one team by five touchdowns. I once saw an article proving by the logic of comparative scores that a small prep school in New Jersey could beat Ohio State 116-0.

Your use of game write-ups and statistics has to go a bit deeper than this to be of any value. If the game you attended is adequately covered, you should be able to check your own interpretation of what you saw. Since the gentlemen of the press write impartially and have the chance to check their information for accuracy, you can probably straighten yourself out on some things that might have seemed puzzling in the swift sequence of events during a game.

Very often some controversial decision by the officials or unusual action by a coach cannot be understood until there is a chance after the game to check with the individuals concerned. Sportswriters are also able to make sure that certain formations or plays were used during the course of a game. It is their job. They know what to look for in advance, and, once again, can have the information checked by press box statisticians and spotters if there is any question.

We have already seen that some writers visit weekday practices in both camps in order to get a good idea of what to look for in the game. Their midweek stories naturally do not divulge a team's planning and strategy. No sportswriter would be able to write authoritative stories for very long if he gained a reputation for not keeping a coach's confidences. This increased knowledge is valuable in the way they can interpret Saturday's game, however, and their midweek stories may be of value in some other respects.

Information on injuries can be helpful, and the more acute experts are able to get across an idea of the mental attitude and psychological fitness of a squad. Quotes from interviews with the coach vary in the amount of information contained in them. Some coaches prefer to talk in generalities, others are frank and open within the dictates of security, and still others, as we have seen, use the opportunity for a little psychological wringing of the "crying towel." Through these articles you may be able to get an idea of a coach's personality and working methods to aid you in estimating what his team will perform in certain situations.

In reading a game write-up, check your own impressions

with those of the writers. If you feel prone to disagree with
the interpretation put on events by one paper, take a look at
other stories about the game and see whether all the writers
are agreed. Usually they are.

In almost every game except a pure runaway, there will
have been some key turning point in the action, some one
play, break, or error of omission that determined the outcome. See if you picked out the same one as the press box
experts. Was it a long pass in a gambling situation, a blocked
kick, a penalty that took the momentum out of what looked
like a touchdown drive, or the exploitation of one weak point,
one spot where a team lacked balance, that swung the tide of
battle? Even in games that end up with a big winning margin, it is possible to see how the fight might have remained
even but for one of these key turning points at an early stage.

If you viewed the game on television, you may have additional questions that need interpreting because of the limitations of the TV coverage, as we have already discussed in
Chapter I. On the other hand, the TV cameras may have
picked up an incident or special play that was completely
missed in the press box.

After a recent big game, one of the most important of that
year, viewed by a nationwide television audience, the referee
arrived home in the evening to be upbraided severely by his
wife, who had seen the game at home, for not calling a flagrant slugging foul that was picked up out of bounds by the
camera. The official had been standing right next to the incident, and yet had not seen it. He was intent on marking the
spot where the play had gone out of bounds, and the camera
angle failed to show that his gaze was not directed at the
fisticuff flurry. The incident also took place too close to the
stands to be seen in the press box. Everyone who saw
the game on television, including the referee's wife, was discussing the affair, and yet not a word appeared about it in any
of the newspaper stories.

This sort of disparity must be taken into consideration in any event reported by eyewitness accounts. It is only with a study of game movies, run repeatedly, that almost everything that happened can be established.

Very few fans have the time or opportunity to study game movies in detail. Since we have said that plain comparative scores are almost worthless, what are the means by which an interested fan can pick out pertinent data from published information?

The statistics box is an important factor. There is a very true saying, in reference to this, that "they don't pay off on first downs." True, a first glance at game statistics showing that one team made 20 first downs to nine for the other team and yet lost the game may seem to make this information unreliable, but the use of the whole set of statistics as printed in newspapers can be very helpful.

Here is an example of a game in which the statistics at first glance might be misleading, and yet they contain the key to the victory.

	Team A	*Team B*
First Downs	18	7
Yards gained rushing	100	144
Yards gained passing	144	94
Passes	30	17
Passes completed	10	7
Passes Intercepted by	1	5
Punts	7	9
Average yards punts	41	38
Fumbles lost	2	3
Yards penalized	30	40

A hasty estimate would indicate a victory by Team A, yet Team B actually pulled a 13-7 upset. The first down advantage of 18-7 obviously was not a deciding factor, so what was? From rushing yardage, it can be seen that Team B did a good job of holding its stronger rivals on the ground, forcing Team A to pass a lot. Team B did give up some damaging yardage in this department but still did an outstanding job of pass defense by confining completion percentage to one third and intercepting five. This might indicate a packed ground defense which also concentrated on rushing the passer, as was the case.

The teams were fairly even on kicking and on damage suffered from penalties, but, from fumbles lost, it is obvious that five exchanges of the ball by this method could affect the course of a tight game. Since this was a highly emotional battle, fought between old, intra-state rivals, the fumbles could probably be traced to the highly charged feelings of the game.

By careful analysis of figures such as these, several deductions can be made. Sometimes a game write-up from another area of the country will only include a paragraph or two on the score and crowd, and the reader has to make his own analysis in this fashion. When it is an important local game, the write-ups should bear out the statistical interpretation. Before going any further, test yourself on how you think Team B won this game. What is your guess?

Here is what actually happened. Team A, the favorite, was able to move the ball both on the ground and through the air in the middle of the field, but each time the play came near payoff territory, Team B stiffened. Three times it took the ball away on downs inside its 25, and three times more it nipped threats with interceptions before they got that far.

Team A was able to take a 7-0 lead early in the game when it set up a score by passing and made the touchdown on an eight yard reverse. Thereafter it was stopped by a combination of B's stubbornness on the ground and alertness on pass defense. As the statistics showed, B slowed itself with three fumbles, and the game was generally ragged and a bit slow. These fumbles wasted the considerable yardage B made on the ground, and both its scores came as the result of breaks. It recovered one fumble on A's six yard line in the second

period, and late in the fourth quarter intercepted a gambling
pass deep in A's territory. Once again Team B ended up
with the ball on the six yard line of Team A through a break,
and it forged the winning score from there.

If you are particularly interested in a team, try a form of
scouting with scissors and paste by collecting its game statistics throughout a season. Putting them in sequence, or com-
piling them into a summary, can produce a very revealing
"form sheet" on a team's general strength and weakness. Taking into consideration the caliber of opposition and the
weather conditions encountered, this sort of compilation
should give answers to some important questions.

Does the team favor passing or running in its attack?
Which type of game has gone better against it? Does it fumble often? How many passes per game does it have intercepted? Is it weak in punting? Has it "out-statisticked" the
opposition and yet compiled a losing record?

Unfortunately, newspapers do not have space for a more
complete set of statistics, and they have standardized a form
that leaves out the number of running plays, yardage on punt,
kickoff and pass interception returns, and punts blocked.
Knowing these added facts can give an even clearer picture of
how a team operated and why a game was won.

An indication of what balance between running and passing a team uses can be gained without knowing the number
of running plays, simply through examining the number of
passes thrown. In college football, anywhere between fifteen
and twenty-five passes thrown is a fairly normal dependence
on this weapon as a balancing threat for the running game and
for producing scores. If the figure is over twenty-five, you
can generally deduce that the team was putting overbalance
on its passing, either in an attempt to spring an upset over a
potentially stronger foe, or to exploit an already discovered
weakness.

Should you find a team habitually throwing a lot of passes

no matter what the caliber of the opposition, it is a good bet that the coach's personality and mode of thinking tend to the aerial game, and that he has an above-average passer to use. Check your own team's pass defense if a squad like this is on the schedule. Also check the defenses your coach may devise for the occasion. Often a team that puts too much emphasis on one phase of the game, no matter how successfully, can eventually be stopped by special treatment.

Another dangerous opponent is the team with a losing record and impressive statistics. Pure comparative scores may indicate an easy game coming up, until it is seen that the team habitually charges up and down the field between the twenty yard lines, piling up big yardage only to lose out on fumbles, penalties or interceptions. Some day this team is going to stop giving games away, pull itself together and harness its power properly. Your team had better be forewarned that an explosion is imminent. Overconfidence can be a very dangerous factor in this sort of situation.

Here again, however, careful pre-game strategic planning can take advantage of a team prone to these faults. Knowing that an opponent has been wasting power and throwing away chances with jittery actions, a coach can build his game plans around these traits, using the psychological factor to his team's advantage. If your paperwork "scouting" has indicated a situation like this, keep an eye peeled for your team's efforts to throw the erratic team off balance.

Why not try to make up a general "scouting report" on a future opponent by this method, using only publicly available data? It can add immeasurably to your interest in and satisfaction from the actual game when you see it, and it can give more meat and meaning to the newspaper write-ups you study.

Here is a check list of some facts you can pick out of Sunday and midweek newspaper stories to help you know what to look for and expect when you take your seat in the stadium:

Type of offensive formation
Use of more than one offensive formation
Unusual shifts
Type of game favored: running or passing
Most frequently used passer; ball carrier
Defensive strengths and weaknesses
Punting proficiency: frequency
Proneness to fumbling and penalties
Length of tenure of coach
Dependence on individual stars
Place kicking proficiency: kickoffs, goals, extra points
Familiarity with opposition
Playing at home or away
Climate at home: altitude, heat; changes if travelling
Importance of game on schedule (and traditionally)
Caliber of schedule
Class predominance on squad: sophomore, junior or senior?

These are not listed in order of importance, as the factors vary in each case, but they should all be considered in your pre-game estimates, along with any other more exact details of organization and operation you can gather.

With all this, your careful analysis may prove to be completely cockeyed when the final results are in. Don't let that worry you; so are those of many of the professional "experts." Football would lose much of its fascination if there were never any upsets, and every fan can remember some stirring occasions when the results went completely against all logic. Sometimes careful planning brought it about, and on other occasions that overworked but still heartbreakingly true cliché that "footballs take funny bounces" was the answer. Or it may have been the equally obvious fact that the mental processes of young men under the pressure of competition sometimes take funny bounces too.

When you have witnessed a genuine upset, your ability to

figure out *how* it came about, and *why*, should add to your appreciation of future contests. When an underdog has pulled off an amazing form reversal, was it really a fluke, a "funny bounce of the ball," or was it the result of some careful planning by the winning coach to take advantage of some hitherto unexploited weakness of the favored team? Did the surprise winner use some new offensive formation or suddenly switch a predominantly running game to passing? Did it overbalance its defense to play to the strength of the opposition, "giving away" some other phase of play, and get away with the gamble? Was the previous success of the favored team based on the exploits of an outstanding star, who had an off day or was bottled up by a special stratagem?

In the preceding pages of this book, we have outlined to you the details of how this type of special adjustment can be made and have shown you the scouting, planning, coaching and quarterbacking methods that produced them. Use of the procedure described for watching a game properly by "not watching the ball" should have enabled you to pick them out visually. In fact, perhaps you are by now even ahead of the Sunday papers in your knowledge of what went on afield.

There is another form of "paperwork" you might want to try in order to get more pleasure out of a game. Perhaps you have noticed, usually in Monday editions, that some papers print animated charts of the action of an important game on the previous Saturday. Most reporters use a similar chart to follow the game they are covering, finding it easier and quicker to refer back to than a bundle of notes. They don't draw comic pictures of ball carriers and mascots around the fringes, but they do keep a complete record of the game action in this way, supplemented by their own code of notes and symbols near important plays to bring out any special information.

Rabid baseball fans like to keep their own box score, and keeping a football chart is something of the same sort of play-by-play record. A cold stadium, with fans jumping up and down and the wind whistling around you is not the best place in the world for paper work, and you may find it hard to keep a chart under these circumstances. Given a nice day and a little elbow room, you could possibly keep one by inserting a blank piece of paper in your program; or, if you want to look very businesslike, bring a clipboard along with you.

More likely, however, keeping a chart would be easier and more rewarding if you were listening to a game on the radio or watching it on television. This graphic outline of the ebb and flow of play brings a game into much sharper focus in every way.

The accompanying illustration, (Diagram 37) is just such a chart of the 1946 Penn-Princeton game, the famous 17-14 upset that we still look upon at Princeton as one of the high points of our coaching regime. The key at the bottom gives the simple symbols necessary for keeping track of the play. There is no rule on any of this. Simply use symbols that are clear to you. More can be added, such as an indication of where first downs were gained and differentiation between types of kicks.

You will note that the chart does not indicate lateral movement of the ball. This would make it too jumbled and crisscrossed to read. As shown here, it merely gives yards gained and type of play, running or passing. There is nothing to stop you from adding all the data you want, "r.e.," "l.t.," etc., to indicate the hole through which the play went, whether it was a reverse or straight play, and who made the tackle. On the illustration, not all the plays are identified as to ball carrier, especially on short gains. To save space and provide for this, you could use program numbers instead of names to indicate the players, and make a note as well of the tackler and key blocker. It might also be a good idea to record the score and time of game at the point of each touchdown or field goal.

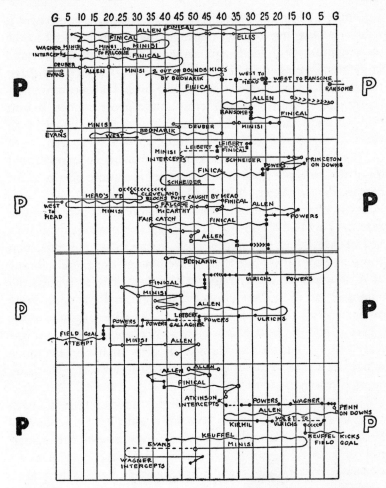

KEY

- o PENN'S BALL
- • PRINCETON'S BALL
- ▫ INCOMPLETE PASS
- — RUNNING PLAY
- ~ KICK
- --- PASS
- >>>> PENALTY

NOV. 2, 1946

PRINCETON 17

PENN 14

Diagram 37—Game Chart of Pennsylvania vs. Princeton, 1946

Football being the immensely variegated game it is, there is a never ending list of items that could be checked to fill in the picture more completely and enhance your appreciation and understanding of it. The serious student, given a good game to get his teeth into, could go on and on in his search for pertinent and interesting detail. Just as the great concert pianist will tell you that one of the major fascinations of his art lies in the fact that he never stops learning, so will a football coach tell you that you can never learn all there is to know about the game. Deeper knowledge just provides more of a base for further development. It is that kind of a sport.

Because of the constant challenge it offers, because its possibilities for innovation and experimentation are inexhaustible, and because there are satisfactions in the watching, coaching and playing of the game that go far beyond the mere winning of it, football has a major role in the American scene. Its demands on an individual's loyalty, courage, self-reliance, sense of fairness and cooperation, and ability to bear up under the severest kind of physical and mental pressures have been transferred to a code for a whole way of life that has meant much in the history of our country. Belittled by some, scoffed at by others, misunderstood by many more, football has been abused, exploited, over-emphasized and under-emphasized with a vigor and sincerity that have only gone to prove its importance and to show the real grip it does have on the American public.

Because it is such a great game, and because we want you to share its entertainment, excitement, drama, its matching of wits and a multitude of other intangible rewards, we hope this book has helped to make you more familiar with its many fascinating aspects.

THE END